THE PLAYS OF JOHN WHITING

THE PLAYS OF
JOHN WHITING

An Assessment

SIMON TRUSSLER

LONDON
VICTOR GOLLANCZ LTD
1972

ISBN 0 575 00725 7

Printed in Great Britain by
The Camelot Press Ltd, London and Southampton

To

JOAN AND JOHN

with love and gratitude

Contents

Acknowledgements

Parts of this book first appeared in the *Tulane Drama Review* during 1966, and are included here by courtesy of the editor. Excerpts from the plays of John Whiting are reprinted by kind permission of Mrs Asthorne Lloyd Whiting and Heinemann Educational Books. The page references in the text are to the two volumes of *The Collected Plays of John Whiting*, edited by Ronald Hayman, to whom my thanks are due for making available an early proof of this edition, and, in the fifth chapter, to the two collections of Whiting's prose, *The Art of the Dramatist* and *John Whiting on Theatre*, published by Alan Ross, to whom I am obliged for permission to reproduce extracts.

INTRODUCTION

Introduction

JOHN WHITING, in a tragically brief career as a playwright interrupted for several years by disillusion with the live theatre and soon afterwards by death, had just a single West End success—with his last completed play, *The Devils*. His earlier work had aroused fierce antagonism and fiercer enthusiasm, but more often in print than on the stage: and even when *Saint's Day* achieved its long-awaited London revival in 1965, long after Whiting's name had won its place in the drama textbooks, the play continued to baffle critics and audiences, and closed after only a brief run.

Anyone coming fresh to his plays and their history might, then, be forgiven for thinking them the work of a closet dramatist—citing in support a structural and thematic density (at least in the first three plays) too complex to be disentangled in the immediacy of production. Yet it has always been the practical men and women of the theatre who have championed Whiting, and been the first to understand what he was getting at and to defend him from the charges of obscurantism levelled by newspaper reviewers and academic critics alike.[1] Maybe this is because it is the practitioner who has the better chance of growing gradually into a play, as if it were a second skin: whilst the professional critic, though he ought to be able to distinguish a performance which baffles an actor from one which merely baffles *him*, too often lets his notice become simply a sounding board for his own preconceptions.

In fact, the enjoyment and enrichment to be derived from Whiting's best work has less to do with its stageworthiness *as such*, than with how much trouble one is prepared to take over assimilating and preferably repeating the experience it has to offer, on stage *or* page. And this, in turn, has to do with a kind of drama—Pinter's *The Birthday Party*, Arden's *Serjeant Musgrave's Dance* and Wesker's *The Friends* are of the company—which is too closely textured to get across to any but the most alert of audiences at a first acquaintance, yet which is found to be more and more fruitful the better one gets to know it. Lacking, as we do, an adequate descriptive grammar of modern drama—an equivalent, say, to Wayne C. Booth's brilliant *Rhetoric of Fiction*—it is impossible here to do more than mention the problem, which is really one for the aesthetic theorist: yet it surely touches the critical response at a traditionally sore spot, and may help to explain the apparently greater insensitivity of theatre reviewers towards originality when it is compounded with opacity.

This rewarding ambiguity is not a matter of identifiable themes or particular preoccupations—least of all those that have come to be associated with the "new English dramatists" Whiting is often said to foreshadow. He was never among the "committed" writers of the late 1950s, who crusaded for proletarian culture and against the bomb. Instead, he claimed conscious and instinctive allegiance to an older tradition—the tradition of an intellectual elite, whose business was to write difficult plays for a discriminating audience. Maybe such an audience never really existed: certainly, Whiting never made contact with it. Yet his recurrent concern with the nature of violence and the limits of personal responsibility anticipated the interest of a

younger generation of dramatists in conflicts less immediately
accessible than those of the bedroom and the kitchen sink.
Among the writers assessed in the present series of studies,
he is, then, closest in sympathy to Pinter, though he admired
the political ambiguity of John Arden's early work.[2] And
he had no time at all for what he regarded as the simplistic
solutions proposed by Arnold Wesker—in his politics if not
always, he conceded, in his plays.[3]

But if the terrorising of a hapless victim in Whiting's
Conditions of Agreement foreshadows the theme of Pinter's *The
Birthday Party*, and the warped yet ruthless logic of *Saint's
Day* is akin to the insane reasoning of Arden's Serjeant
Musgrave, there is nothing in Whiting's most overtly political
play, *Marching Song*, to suggest the playwright's personal
commitment to a cause or a country. Rather, Whiting stands
scrupulously aside from the morality of his characters—the
action becoming almost an ethical microcosm, in which each
can behave as the warp and woof of his individuality dictates. No man in Whiting's plays is his brother's keeper—
at least, not successfully so—yet those who are truest to
themselves, like Dido in *Marching Song*, prove least hurtful
to those about them, whilst those who try to impose a
personal morality upon another's life create a dissociated
havoc that is objectively, and with intentional bathos, often
the product of nothing more than a practical joke.

Beyond defining his own preoccupations—of which
practical joking was certainly one—Whiting did not regard
his plays as in need of explication.[4] But he once wrote—
and the aphorism is helpful in approaching his own work—
that the purpose of entertainment was to reassure, whereas
the purpose of art was to raise doubt:[5] and it is, I think, by
considering just how Whiting's own works raise doubts that
one can best comprehend the density of their structure, the

ambiguity of their themes, and the complexity of their characterisation. Each of his major plays explores not only the responsibility of each man for his actions, but also the premises on which action itself depends. Now absurdist drama, too, explores these premises—but by a process of caricaturing reality, of taking it truly *ad absurdum*. Whiting's work is almost invariably (the exception is the brief one-acter *No Why*) related to a recognisable norm of social behaviour, if only because it is by establishing such a norm that departures from it can best be understood.

In his earliest plays, *Conditions of Agreement* and *Saint's Day*, he used the values of childhood as a chosen point of departure —a kind of subjective correlative—the disproportionate tensions of infancy serving as a framework for the warped inner logic of each work. And so I have taken "Second Childhoods" as a title for the chapter in which these plays are discussed—to reflect both the adult repudiation of adolescence in *Conditions of Agreement*, and the regressive senility of Paul Southman in *Saint's Day*. The remaining chapters shelter under similar umbrella-titles, which hopefully suggest the affinities fully explored in each. Whiting's third play, *A Penny for a Song*, was, however, so distinctive in manner and mood that it demands a short section to itself—its title, "Festive Summer", evocative of the work's even temper as of its time. The austere detachment, alike of mood and physical situation, of *Marching Song* and *The Gates of Summer* sets them, in my third chapter, "Above the Battle", whilst the return to an early theme in Whiting's last plays is reflected in the title of my fourth chapter, "Children of Misfortune". For each of these final works—whether in the enigmatic innocence of Jacob in *No Why*, the crippled immaturity of Peter in *A Walk in the Desert*, or the puerile practical joking that is as central to *The Devils* as it was to

Conditions of Agreement—is again concerned, directly or allusively, with childhood, and, in particular, its apparently unmotivated cruelties.

A fifth chapter, "Doubts and Reassurance", tests Whiting's aphoristic distinction between the purpose of art and of entertainment against his own considerable body of critical writings, and tries to assess the value of his unfashionable view of art as it assisted his own writings, and as it helped him understand the writings of others. But it was only during Whiting's years in the wilderness, and the few years that remained to him afterwards, that his own contemporaries— at least, among his fellow-countrymen—could offer an adequate challenge to his critical or creative capacities: and as a creator, at least, he was doubly unfortunate in anticipating by nearly a decade the new English drama. For not only were his audiences even less ready than they might otherwise have been to meet his demands, but the available influences on which he drew, consciously or unconsciously, for his work in the theatre were particularly unhelpful.

Thus, to think oneself back to the social and theatrical circumstances in which *Saint's Day* was first produced is more fully to understand the puzzled fury which greeted it. The date was September 1951, and the occasion a play competition run by the Arts Theatre Club in London to celebrate the Festival of Britain. It was the year in which the British people were preparing to shake off the trappings of austerity in that gesture of touching if misplaced self-confidence that was to culminate in the restoration of Churchill and the Conservatives to power. *A Penny for a Song*, staged a little more successfully a few months earlier, had certainly been more in tune with such times: but a nation which had just symbolised its hopes in the Dome of Discovery on the South Bank, and seen the insubstantial Skylon soaring purposelessly towards the heavens, was in no mood for the claustrophobic doubts of Whiting's first serious work. In any case, British drama was supposed to be in the throes of a poetic renaissance—the vague spiritual optimism of Eliot's *Cocktail Party* and the civilised whimsy of Christopher Fry's *The Lady's Not For Burning* among its more recent products— whilst the work of Terence Rattigan continued to represent a "realism" that was in fact close in its formal assumptions to the well-made variety William Archer had recommended and Bernard Shaw had rejected half a century earlier.

Sure enough, Whiting's earliest plays contain traces of all three styles—deliberate Eliotian parody in *Saint's Day*, something reminiscent of Fry's more roseate mood in *A Penny for a Song*, and more than a little of Rattigan's mannered colloquialism in *Marching Song*. And later, of course, Brechtian dramaturgy was to affect the form of *The Devils*. Such vestiges are not, in Whiting's case, a product of poetasting—he was, in any case, a greater stage poet than Eliot, Fry or Rattigan—but of a curious eclecticism that infiltrates not just Whiting's style but his often congested content: a jackdaw-like accumulation of detail, often profitable in the richness it yields after successive siftings, yet highlighting in the process the most dated features of the plays, their all-too-discernible literary influences.

Through the dense undergrowth of stylistic embellishment and substantive detail, Whiting directs the almost undeviating narrative line that misguided him into calling his plays "simple"—so that if the process of self-destruction, to cite only his most insistent theme, *were* a simple matter, the description would be apt enough. Of Whiting's six full-length plays, three end in violent death—*Saint's Day* by hanging, *Marching Song* by self-administered poison, *The Devils* by torture and burning at the stake—and three in a reconciliation that is really, except in *A Penny for a Song*, only a proof of inconsequence. Conventionally, in this light, one's expectations might be of a classic approach to dramatic form—the tragic works cathartic, the comic cautionary. Yet the dividing line is curiously narrow, and the impression of leftover lives to kill much the same in *Marching Song* after Rupert's death as in *The Gates of Summer* after the farcical failure of other suicides. In the world of the first play, in the aftermath of war, poison *works*: in the world of the second play, on the brink of war, its identity is merely mistaken. Similarly, *Saint's Day* takes the refusal to recognise personal responsibility to a tragic conclusion, whilst in *A Penny for a Song* a similar refusal is redeemed by good intentions: and in Whiting's earliest work, *Conditions of Agreement*, a practical joke results in a humbling of the human spirit, whilst in his last, *The Devils*, another practical joke results in the extreme physical humiliation of Grandier's brutal putting to death.

This kind of thematic counterpoint recurs at many levels in Whiting's work, and gives it a wholeness—or rather, to avoid prejudging that issue, a consistency—that is perhaps unexpected in a dramatic career so prematurely cut short by death. Or was such a death what had been foreshadowed all along—in the accidental shooting of a young woman in *Saint's Day*, the suicide of a young military hero in *Marching Song*, the sense of satiety in *The Gates of Summer*, the painful death of a worldly priest in *The Devils*? The idea is fanciful, and, in any case, irrelevant to the quality of the plays as works of enduring dramatic art. Yet the apocalyptic quality of so much of Whiting's work, the sense of mortality and the fear of inconsequence that permeates it, encourages if not an affirmative answer to the question at least the frame of mind which tempts one to ask it.

This quality, too, makes it difficult to find an appropriate tone of voice in which to talk of Whiting's work. To say that it generates enthusiasm would be to imply a kind of optimism, or at least a *polemical* pessimism, that just isn't there: yet the qualities which I shall be trying to clarify do leave one with a sense of elevation that is akin to that of Euripidean tragedy—that of the eternally probing, questioning mind, not of the passively resigned fatalist. His plays are hell-fire warnings, yet their tenor is not that of the ranting evangelist provoking to confession and repentance. Rather, it is that of the infinitely compassionate and tolerant man of the world, who has seen too much to tear his hair over mankind's follies, yet foresees so much more that hopeful acceptance does constant battle with despair.

And so one does not write eulogistically of Whiting's work. It would be too much like yelling in a cathedral— an irreverent urge to hear a meaningless echo, when the natural, self-defining need is for an impressed whisper. The sense of inspiration—and of sheer size—are *there*: it is the texture of the masonry, the subtlety of the joints, that renew and make whole again one's admiration after the first, overwhelming impression has been assimilated. But I hope this attitude and emphasis don't lead in the following pages to the feeling that my own admiration for Whiting is muted by anything else but a kind of wondering, exploratory respect—and, occasionally, by the sobering regret that his voice was cut short, like those of so many modern prophets of avoidable doom, by his own early death.

And so, sadly, it is not necessary here to offer the apology made in earlier studies in the present series—that my final chapter should not really be called a Conclusion at all, as it could not be to works on writers with at least half a creative lifetime before them. Yet whatever more Whiting might have achieved had he lived, what he did accomplish had a coherence in creative range and a depth of dramatic insight such as no other playwright of his generation could equal. If he did not prove the source of inspiration to later dramatists that a less austere and isolated writer might have become, he remains potentially the most rewarding of those prophets who have been dishonoured, like Paul Southman in *Saint's Day*, in their own time and country.

Even in the years of belated recognition since his death, there has, however, been relatively little serious critical comment upon Whiting's work—though much casual canonising, which assumes almost in passing his status as a major writer. In attempting this first detailed assessment of his completed plays (I am deliberately ignoring the abandoned work *Noman*, the partial reworking of it as *The Nomads*, and his prolific output of potboiling screenplays),[6] I am not, then, adding to or reacting against a substantial body of critical opinion. And so, whereas in the earlier studies of John Osborne and of Arnold Wesker, it was necessary to put some corrective stress on the psychological insights of reputedly "social" writers, there are, in Whiting's case, relatively few accepted commonplaces to strip away—the single important exception being the tendency to regard *The Devils* as a triumphant breakthrough instead of a not very satisfactory experiment in an unfamiliar form.

The disadvantage of this relative freedom of critical manœuvre is, of course, that the shortage of other writers on Whiting, against whose cross-grained sensibilities my own might helpfully have been sharpened, has no doubt made for some over-simplifications, and even statements of the obvious, in this frankly exploratory work. It is intended as a critical companion to the plays—not as finished literary works, but as raw material for performance. Necessarily, there are gaps that can only be filled in by the work of directors and actors: but hopefully the reader himself will be prepared to follow and challenge the argument, copies of Whiting's plays at hand, with his own creative imagination at work. All quotations in the text from Whiting's plays are accordingly keyed to Ronald Hayman's two-volume collected edition, which is the most readily available both in England and America, though full particulars of other editions of the plays—as of Whiting's non-dramatic published work, and of major critical studies of his writings—will be found in the Bibliography.

Other appendices provide notes and references to the text, cast lists of London productions, and a brief, factual chronology of Whiting's dramatic career—the inclusion of the latter, in Whiting's case, entirely a matter of convenience, not a sly means of avoiding that temptation to interpret plays in a biographical light which can be so dangerously attractive in approaching the work of Osborne and Wesker. My own feeling is that if there exist such associations between Whiting's life and his works, they lie buried too deep for any but the most dedicated biographer to ferret out: in any case, the line of enquiry, intriguing though it might prove, is not one I intend to pursue here.

Not that this absence of obvious personal parallels makes Whiting in any sense an impersonal writer, though he is often an austere one. Indeed, answering criticisms of *Saint's Day*, he once declared that its "so-called symbolism" was really "no more than the use of people, places, things, even ideas and quotations from literature, which have a personal significance, put together to form a whole". Criticism of this method astonished him, for he believed it to be "the natural, indeed fundamental, distinction between art and journalism". But, as he admitted a little later, a play, "unlike a poem or a novel, becomes depersonalised by time and by production".[7] It is, perhaps, this total, chemical change of the often obliquely presented raw material of the mind into that most public of artistic properties, the play in performance, that has worked against easy first receptions of Whiting's work. And in this sense my task in the following pages is to complete the process of depersonalisation, so as to reveal the plays as whole and independent works of art— and, in the case of the major works, to suggest the logical self-sufficiency that allows the worlds they create to become as real and immediate as they are at first glimpse puzzling and unfamiliar. Thus, it is towards a better understanding of the wholeness, independence and self-sufficiency in Whiting's work, and of how it might best be interpreted on the stage, that the present study is dedicated.

THE PLAYS OF JOHN WHITING

Second Childhoods

Conditions of Agreement and *Saint's Day*

CONDITIONS OF AGREEMENT was written in 1948-9, ten years before Pinter's *Birthday Party*: but it was not staged till 1965, and Pinter was unaware of Whiting's first full-length play when planning his own. Yet *Conditions of Agreement*, like *The Birthday Party*, is concerned with the terrorising of a hapless and apparently random victim, and with the staking-out of emotional and territorial claims. Its second act, too, takes the form of a grotesque birthday celebration, in which the chief guest becomes the victim. The crucial difference between the two plays is one of focus—as if Pinter had written *The Birthday Party* from the points of view of Goldberg and McCann instead of the apparently uncomprehending Stanley's.[8] By concentrating on his own pair of plotters Whiting gives added edge to a menace which becomes both more and less explicit. There is no doubt here about the couple's intentions, and if motives are irrational they are no less real: for the comfortably-off retired grocer who has been numbed into passivity by the fall of the final curtain has suffered from childish petulance which has been given grown-up sanction and strength.

The action of the play is set in the living-room of Emily Doon's house "in a small town near Oxford". [5] The original elegance of the place is not quite as decayed as that of Paul Southman's retreat in *Saint's Day*, but there is the same sense of incongruity between a former rococo grandeur and trifling evidences of poverty or neglect—the cheap alarm clock, [5] the kettle, the spirit lamp which doesn't work. [7] Emily's widowhood is one of ill-concealed penury: but it is just enough concealed for her wealthy and evidently adoring neighbour, known only as A.G., never to think of offering financial aid. For this neglect—a symptom of insensitivity rather than meanness—he is hated by Emily's son Nicholas, who, as the play begins, is expected home from honeymoon with his wife Patience. But on his return Nicholas finds an ally, who transforms his vaguely hostile intentions towards A.G. into an active though covert aggressiveness. This ally is Peter Bembo, one-time lover of Emily's, and now back from self-imposed exile in search, it seems, of his past and its friendships.

So far, so straightforward—indeed, almost too straightforward, as the setting-up of a well-made problem play tends to be. But thus to summarise the action is to ignore those coincidental, certainly surreal and often macabre elements which shadow each step in its unfolding. Bembo, as his name suggests, was once a famous clown: his fifteen-year absence has been spent, inexplicably, in Armenia, and he has lost one eye. Nicholas, too, has been maimed—by the loss of a leg. And A.G. is spiritually crippled, obsessed with the manner of his wife's death—a fatal fall, head-first, from precarious scaffolding, agonisingly yet comically prolonged by one of her feet catching in its framework, the woman's skirts tumbling about her head. [15] The scaffolding supported the seats of a Spanish circus, and in this Spanish circus Bembo was performing as the provincial grocer's wife dangled and fell, indelibly staining the retina of her widower's mind with a memory he has tried at once to perpetuate and to exorcise in verbal reminiscence. And so Bembo, discovering the coincidence, seeks revenge against the one person who has shed tears that were not of laughter at his clowning—whereas Nicholas merely wants to hurt a man who is too insensitive to recognise his mother's need for hard cash. The form of their joint attack is to undermine A.G.'s confidence in himself, by undermining his belief in the manner of his wife's death. And just as Paul Southman's birthday was to become the day of his destruction in *Saint's Day*, the day of A.G.'s humiliation is also the anniversary of his wife's birth.

It would be an understatement to say that this marks out difficult territory for any dramatist to tread. Whiting's deliberately tortuous scenario, lacking the imprecision of Pinter's menace, could easily have become absurd in an all too conventional sense. In fact, the gothick proportions the play does assume are carefully modulated by the tone of voice of the storyteller. For, as so often in Whiting's work, one is intensely conscious of the teller in the tale—not as a deliberately interruptive device, as he is employed in brechtian dramaturgy, but as an omnipresent creative consciousness, which makes one aware of every speech and every development in the action simultaneously as something that is told and as a mode of telling: the effect is to infuse even the most melodramatic moment with its cool irony. And only very occasionally does this become over-obtrusive. When Emily imagines that Nicholas is about to commit suicide, she tells Patience that they "must not obstruct his designs or we shall distort the pattern of our lives". [67] Now this *is* Whiting indulging in double-bluff, for Nicholas has no intention of killing himself, and his mother's metaphysics become at once pretentious and unsubtly ironic: the trick is too clever to deceive the ear.

But usually Whiting retains perfect command over his tones of voice—here, for instance, Emily is recalling her first meeting with Peter Bembo, at a party for crippled children:

> And you said, "How d'you do," and stood on your head.
> Your trousers slipped down to your knees and showed your
> yellow socks. I stood before you, your face at my feet,
> with my hand stretched out like a fool. All around us the
> children laughed and clattered their little wooden legs. [9]

The last sentence is extraordinarily right: the sound of the words, changing at the connective from the rippling to the harsh, echoes the sick cheerfulness of the image. The whole speed is more reminiscent of first-person narrative than of dramatic dialogue, and its tendency to slip into a slightly distanced retrospection is one to which many of Whiting's characters are prone. It is, moreover, insistent in its allusiveness to the rest of the play. The clown's trousers falling about his knees, even Emily's hand stretched out uselessly towards him, reduce *ad absurdum* the already bathetic image of A.G. twittering helplessly as his wife, upside down too, is about to fall: and around both the laughter of children surges. The cripples have wooden legs, like Nicholas. They laugh, like him, at childish things. And so on: as in many of the speeches, there is a collapsing inwards towards the dense core of the play, and this at once exemplifies and predicts the manner in which its every vital action resolves, ultimately, into childishness.

Seen in this light, even the recurrent and otherwise inexplicable business with a reading lamp becomes purposeful. The lamp is one specially adapted by Nicholas, which refuses to work when Emily lends it to A.G. His returning the gadget gets him over the threshold for the first time in the play, [11] and after its final words have been spoken one of Emily's last actions is to put the lamp away in a cupboard. [81] A.G. is preoccupied with his failure to get the thing to work—an obsession no less trivial than the pettish causes of Peter and Nicholas's hatred. Each character either really behaves like an overgrown child, or is accused by the others of doing so. It's as if the participants in some playground game of grown-ups had perpetuated its half-formed fantasies about adult life into the relationships of their supposed maturity: in consequence, they are crippled both physically and mentally. Even Helen, A.G.'s wife, has been found to be infertile just before her death, and Nicholas's lost leg is an obvious enough castration-symbol—indeed, it would be much too obvious, did not such symbolism transcend and transmute the whole play. For everything relates to and reinforces it—even Peter's obsession with *not crying* has its brave-little-manly overtones of the nursery, and Nicholas's threat of suicide is no more than a petulant, infantile practical joke.

It's easy to impose a meaning on any play as closely-textured as this: but here the interpretation is carefully and continuously verified by both the words and the action. Consider each of the characters and their relationships—the *least* evidently childish first. Patience, indeed, is the most nearly adult among them, and, no doubt for this reason, is repeatedly accused of childishness by the others—most pointedly, at the curtain of the second act. [60] Nicholas wants her ordered to bed—like a disobedient toddler—when she begins to assert herself, [74] and even A.G. excuses a reaction he has wrongly interpreted by blaming her youth for *her* "misunderstanding". [78]

Patience usually—dare one add *patiently*—accepts the

role in which she has been cast: indeed, she is deceived by
the superficial sophistication of the menage into which she
has married. Here, Nicholas asks her what she has been
thinking as she sits, awkwardly apart from the conversation,
and her reply is that of the bored child—or of the unself-
conscious adult:

> Oh, I don't know. Why Mr. Bembo wears that black
> patch over his eye. Whether I should call your mother Mrs.
> Doon or Mother or what. Whether I couldn't have some
> more sugar in my tea—I like a lot of sugar in my tea. And
> I was thinking about you. [27]

She is "on sure, known ground", directs Whiting, in talking
about her own sexual feelings, [28] but she is incapable of
entering vicariously into the experience of others: and in
this sense, she is a sort of immature, inward-looking version
of Dido in *Marching Song*. True, Dido is a dropout and
Patience a respectable working-class girl who can't quite
forget her days in service; but they share a spontaneity of
sexual gesture—indeed, of anything to do with their own
physicality—which does something to restore Rupert Forster's
self-awareness in *Marching Song*, and which contrasts with
Nicholas's infantile sexuality here.

The contrast is strongest when Nicholas reacts with splen-
etic fury to the news that Patience has packed up all the
old books and toys in their now common bedroom—an act
which he interprets as a betrayal of his own childhood, while
he mouths platitudes about the sacredness of other people's
property. [46–8] Such double-talk is typical of Nicholas.
He enjoys making over-assertive generalisations—his supposed dislike of diminutives, for example—and then sulking
when he's caught betraying his own spur-of-the-moment

principle. [21] It's all part of [his schoolboy complexion.

Not only the *causes* of Peter and Nicholas's hatred of A.G. are trivial: so also are the means by which they express it. Exploiting his morbid fears at the beginning of act two, Nicholas is quite pertinently told to "grow up", [32] and Peter and he conspire together like a pair of adolescents. They settle on the practical joke of an anonymous threatening letter as their first act of defiance: if this doesn't work, perhaps poisoned chocolates will prove more effective. [40-1] And just as Nicholas covers up his own childishness by accusing Patience of being a child, [47] so he reacts defensively to a comparison which Peter suggests between A.G.'s anger and childish defiance:

NICHOLAS: Tell me, Peter, were you really amused by A.G.'s defiance just now?
PETER: Not amused. Touched.
NICHOLAS: Do you mean emotionally moved?
PETER: Yes. Children——
NICHOLAS: I know nothing about children.
PETER: No. Well, children have the same quality of defiance. I remember once——
NICHOLAS: Are you defending A.G.?
PETER: No. I remember I——
NICHOLAS: The defiance of children, I should imagine, is always in defence of their integrity.
PETER: It is with child or man. [41]

Quite. A little too pat, really. Nicholas has even described his eavesdropping upon A.G. as "presumably the child in the adult—the child playing a silent, lonely and mysterious game". [36] But Peter is not unaware of the irony, and a little later manipulates it in the course of forgiving Nicholas's doubts about his own loyalty. "It is understandable, this—defiance. Not only your leg lets you down, eh?" [44]

Peter, although he selects just the right word for Nicholas's attitude after that carefully punctuated pause, is no less capable of childishness. Long ago, A.G. broke his own mysterious taboo against tears. And so Peter trips him up and pretends it was an accident [49]—declaring, in rebuttal of A.G.'s accusations:

> I have nothing against you personally—and if I had anything against you I'd not play schoolboy tricks on you. I am not in any way a malicious person. [50]

Peter *does* have something against A.G., of course. He *is* a malicious person. And his malice *does* show itself in schoolboy tricks. He urges A.G. to "start a charity fund for crippled children", [52] but the symbolically castrated Nicholas is not the only cripple still hobbling about in an emotional nursery.

The theme of Whiting's television play, *A Walk in the Desert*, which nobody but the playwright himself could have regarded as a revamping of his first work,[9] does nevertheless display certain similarities. In both works, a cripple plays a vicious practical joke on an unwitting victim, and blames his parents—though in Nicholas's case only a mother is available—for his own personal shortcomings. *Conditions of Agreement* is thus complicated not only by the earthy innocence of Patience but also by the matriarchal grandeur of Emily. One senses that she is, indeed, in some measure to blame for her son's inadequacy: but, apart from hints of Nicholas's adolescent disgust at her succession of lovers and of his resentment at the parlour tricks he was expected to perform for them, [19–20] there is little attempt to clarify her present feelings, and her eventual role in the action turns out to be a more minor one than her big opening scene with the newly-arrived Peter and A.G. seemed to anticipate.

Perhaps she is Stella in *Saint's Day*—that play was already in progress when *Conditions of Agreement* was completed—casting her shadow before. So many of Whiting's characters do seem to spawn spiritual progeny—and there is a painting of her beside the fireplace, [5] mirroring a younger self now unrecognised by Peter, just as Charles Heberden's picture resurrects the dead Stella in oils. Like Stella, too, Emily is a passionately involved spectator of events which she finds herself powerless to comprehend or control.

This similarity shouldn't be pushed too far, for such significance as it has surely relates to Whiting's tendency to be haunted by particular scenes, personalities or moods until he has perfectly transmuted them into dramatic form, and not to *Conditions of Agreement* as such. This does, though, perhaps explain why Emily seems so forceful yet so unsatisfactory a figure—her function and felt dramatic presence almost evaporating during the last act, as it moves towards the final terrorising of A.G. If she *has* a consistent function, it is catalytic: she has made Nicholas what he is, yet is an entirely passive observer of his actions; she has attracted both Peter Bembo and A.G. to her home, yet is set quite apart from the chain of events which links them. But not even in this sense does she add up to a very satisfactory character.

Even A.G.'s dead wife Helen fits more comprehensibly into what turns out to be the developing pattern of the action than does Emily. Indeed, the marriage of Helen and A.G. is a kind of might-have-been paradigm for the play—and, like a paradigm, its story is repeated instinctively, almost parrot-fashion, by A.G. at the slightest opportunity. He was ten years older than his wife, whilst Nicholas is five years Patience's senior. Helen worked in a grocer's shop, Patience was a housemaid. Both Nicholas and A.G. are contemptuous of circuses, yet Helen, says her widower, displayed "an almost childlike understanding of the clown's antics". [14] And Patience, too, responds to the immediacy of the tangible, shrinking from her husband's preoccupation with the past:

> You see, Nicholas, I can never imagine old, cold bodies doing what we've done, can you? It's like a true story I once read of two people in love, loving. It wasn't until the end of the book I found out they were both dead and that made it horrible. [28]

This, also, is paradigmatic. A.G.'s obsessive repetitions of *his* story of a dead love and a dead lover suffuse the whole play with a remembrance of decaying bones which once stirred warm and sensuous flesh; and, suggestively enough, Emily's choice of a poet to read aloud to Patience is John Donne. [62]

Similarly, Bembo's presence—A.G. had thought *he* was dead [12]—triggers off all Nicholas's resentment against his mother's succession of ageing lovers. Anally obsessive about accounting for his money and hoarding his possessions, Nicholas accumulates the relics of the past about him yet purports to despise childish things as much as cast-off lovers. Patience, more truly childlike, lives spontaneously in the present-tense of her physical sensations. It's as if every character in the play were consciously or unconsciously claiming allegiance to past or present, youth or age, living at first hand or at second. This is not necessarily anything to do with *being* young or old. Emily has no hesitation in declaring that she doesn't like her own son, [9] but Peter, at sixty-eight quite old enough to be Nicholas's grandfather, wins his confidence through his own adolescent manners of speech and of response.

It's been remarked that the tone of many of the exchanges in *Conditions of Agreement* anticipates theatre of the absurd, and that the play is a comedy of menace before its time.[10] This is true enough. But it's true precisely because "absurdity" in this sense is so often marked by a reversion to the illogic and the exaggerated yet terribly real emotions of childhood, the surfacing of long-sublimated desires; and because "menace" is so often marked by the arbitrariness— the random picking of the innocent victim—of street-corner bullying. Read the long, overlapping dialogue in which Peter and Nicholas bolster each other's confidence as they sap A.G.'s, [56–8] or the more direct—yet in substance equally ambiguous—onslaught upon him in the last act. The idiom, certainly, is that of absurdist drama: but the tactics are those of ten-year-old toughs. It is in the inconsequence of these characters' *motives*, indeed of their lives, that the real absurdity of the play lies.

A.G.'s wife was killed in an absurd, unnecessary accident. Nicholas's leg was not really lost in the war, as he likes people to think, and has become merely a good excuse for habitual laziness. [23] How Peter lost an eye makes no more than "a long and, I think, very funny story". [7] Emily's own, scarcely mentioned husband did, apparently, die a hero's death: but Peter's slight deafness comes on at any mention of heroism, and Emily's repetition of the tale, in a louder voice, makes it ludicrous. [8] A.G. is a grocer, Peter is a clown, Patience is a parlourmaid, Emily is a faded fortune-hunter, and Nicholas is nothing. If there is purpose or feeling in the whole bunch, it manifests itself only in trivial acts of aggression towards others, or, in

Patience's case, in self-absorption. Even death itself is reduced to a practical joke. Peter persuades A.G. that his wife's death was one of suicidal desperation instead of a stupid accident; and the absent Nicholas taunts his mother and wife with his threat to take his own life.

In conclusion, consider this exchange, in which Emily is trying to make allowances for her son:

EMILY: Nicholas——

PATIENCE: Yes?

EMILY: He has suffered great disappointment.

PATIENCE: Yes?

EMILY: It is only human.

PATIENCE: You mustn't talk to me like that. Human. Men and women do this and that. I am myself and I behave as Patience Loratt—Patience Doon. He is Nicholas Doon and as Nicholas Doon he must be expected to behave. I don't need excuses for him. (*She pauses.*) Go on. (*She pauses.*) Go on!

EMILY: He is going to kill himself. (*She goes quickly on.*) Himself. Nicholas. Himself. He says he intends to kill himself. It is part of a plan that I don't understand: to kill himself. Do you believe me? Do you, child?

PATIENCE: Child! I am a child and you make fun of my innocence.

EMILY: No!

PATIENCE: I meant——

EMILY: I'll forget that you're a child. I'll ignore your innocence.

PATIENCE: I meant to say ignorance. I am not innocent. I am foul. [65]

The dividing line between innocence and ignorance, experience and enervation, naïvety and narcissism: the play is about apparently abstract distinctions such as these. Abstract, because the characters and the situations embodying the issues are so pathetically inconsequential: and this very inconsequence throws back the attention upon the qualities as such.

Conditions of Agreement is an extraordinarily complex play—perhaps unnecessarily so in its surface action, for it is *beneath* the surface of this action that Whiting weaves, with unnerving dispassion, the web of relationships, and of interlocking ambitions and shared fears, which can be traced there in psychologically assured relief. His "conditions of agreement" ally an old man and a young one against a middle-aged grocer: whilst the evocative, compellingly selfish character of Patience makes emotional terms of her own. The play is theatre of the absurd because it is too obviously symbolic to be satisfying merely in its symbolism, and too trivial in the minutiae of its complicated plotting to matter as a problem play. What remains is a study of emotions in the abstract—as bafflingly banal to the unsympathetic adult mind as a childhood storm in a teacup, but no less sharply felt at the exposed nerve ends.

Saint's Day—begun, before *Conditions of Agreement*, in 1947, completed two years later, and stormily staged at the Arts Theatre in 1951—is even more allusive, even more densely packed, than *Conditions of Agreement*. And if it is possible in the earlier play to refer the complexity back to a single dominant motif—emotional growth stunted at adolescence —in *Saint's Day* there is no such common denominator, although Whiting's original introduction pinned down its theme, with unwonted explicitness, as "self-destruction".[11] But in this same note Whiting confessed to the play's "accumulation of detail", and in a later interview he attributed this to the fact that it was essentially a personal and (more especially) a technical exercise. "I think everybody writes one play," he continued, "on which he then draws technically for the rest of his life. You have on paper a sort of anthology of what you can do."[12] Whether, in these circumstances, one has also on paper—let alone on stage—a play which is meaningful in its own right is more open to doubt. In the event, the complications of *Saint's Day* largely transcend their formally-conscious origins: and if they throw off a profusion of tangents to the play's professed main theme of self-destruction, at least the tangents do actually touch the inner circle of the play, not merely dart tantalisingly but inconclusively towards it.

There is, however, one exception, one unfortunate tendency towards incoherence. In *Conditions of Agreement* Whiting had tried to wring more rhetoric out of Nicholas's threatened suicide than it turned out to be worth. And here, in parodistic vein,[13] he is sometimes prone to slip into the line-stressed periods of Eliot's later verse plays with similarly portentous effect:

Careful! We are approaching the point of deviation. At one moment there is laughter and conversation and a progression: people move and speak smoothly and casually, their breathing is controlled and they know what they do. Then there occurs a call from another room, the realization that a member of the assembly is missing, the sudden shout into the dream and the waking to find the body with the failing heart lying in the corridor—with the twisted limbs at the foot of the stairs—the man hanging from the beam, or the child floating drowned in the garden pool. Careful! Be careful! We are approaching that point. The moment of the call from another room. [132]

Now this is admittedly attention-focusing. But not only is it uneasy on the contemporary ear, it is fraudulently ambiguous in its semantics: and granted that it *is* an intended parody, its failure to fit meaningfully into the context of the play's action suggests that it is a serious artistic mistake. Consider too this later speech:

Somewhere here there is a link—Think, John Winter, think! What did he say to Paul? What did he say to the old woman? Is it contained in that? I don't know. Perhaps so simple. No, we've missed the moment for discovery. It was when she said, "He spoke to me." Gone now. Never mind. Doesn't matter. [153]

These points-of-deviation and moments-of-discovery don't matter indeed. And their intrusion is not only irrelevant but purposelessly distracting. If *Saint's Day* has its identifiable turning points and moments of truth—and it does—they aren't to be pinned down in verbal parlour-games such as these.

Defending the allusive elements in his play, Whiting remarked that its "so-called symbolism" was "no more than the use of people, places, things, even ideas and quotations from literature, which have a personal significance, put together to form a whole".[14] Yes: but how is such dense fabric of *personal* allusion to be made meaningful in a stage production—such as, admittedly, Whiting never thought the play would achieve? As it happened, his theatrical instinct ensured that *Saint's Day* should have more than "personal significance". Even certain of the exercises in comparative technique—notably the shaping of the last act into the form of a mock-classical tragedy—succeed because, although they may have begun as authorial sports, their inspiration

has evidently sprung from and connected with the action—
and not merely been, as in the case of the more stridently
Eliotian passages, a bright idea lathered on from outside.

As happens in *Conditions of Agreement*, an audience for
Saint's Day is required to acclimatise itself to a slightly
unexpected setting before anything very positive happens.
The curtain rises, and light is shed gradually on a set which
is resonant with surreal ambiguities. Represented is the
living room in the now decrepit home of Paul Southman.
The place is "an architectural freak": its furnishings are "of
excellent quality", but they have "lost their grace by neglect
and misuse". A bicycle lies upstage, its pump detached, and
half-light filters through drawn curtains on to a cavernous
stairway. [91] The scene is one of arbitrary and *incongruous*
neglect: it is as if a staid habit of living had been shifted
slightly out-of-focus, partly from choice and partly from
poverty-stricken necessity. Similarly, one is forced into a
visual double-take at the opening of the third act, when
refugees from the village have added their own accumulation
of "surprising objects taken by those flying from a catastrophe" [148] to the jumble on stage.

Unadorned, a plot summary makes even stranger reading
than a synopsis of *Conditions of Agreement*. Paul Southman,
once famous as a "pamphleteer and lampoonist, poet and
revolutionary" but now approaching senility, has lived in
self-imposed exile for twenty-five years—an exile to which he
retreated after the concerted attacks of the literary world
upon his controversial pamphlet *The Abolition of Printing*
(a title with a prophetically, but as it turns out non-
significantly, McLuhanite ring). Southman is cared for by his
grand-daughter Stella Heberden, her young artist husband
Charles, and a loyal though apparently unpaid manservant
called John Winter. His attacks upon society have become,

of necessity, microcosmic: the microcosm is the nearby village, and its inhabitants react as society reacted, with an active hatred born of incomprehension.

The action takes place on 25th January, the poet's eighty-third birthday, [99] and also, eponymously, the anniversary of the conversion of St Paul. On this day Southman is to be taken to London, to be feted by a literary establishment which no longer feels it fashionable to vilify him. But John Winter returns from the village, where he has been sent to beg more credit for food, with startling news:

> Three private soldiers have escaped from a detention camp. They have made their way to the village, and it is believed they slept last night in the village hall. This morning, at an early hour, they broke out of the hall and began marauding and looting the village. Although unarmed they terrorised the villagers. Having obtained food they retired, and are now hiding at some place in the surrounding country. [112]

The context of this speech is carefully exploited: it immediately follows a sequence of short and overlapping domestic exchanges, so that its formality—odd anyway in the usually taciturn manservant—is the more marked in contrast. Indeed, attention is drawn to it by Southman's solemn thanks for an "excellent and lucid report". Thus, typically, is formal parody—the impersonal military reportage of the speech—integrated with the mood of the action, as it changes here from household bickering to quasi-military campaigning. Southman recognises the escaped soldiers as potential allies against the real "enemy", the village: but to Stella the plotting amounts to no more than two old men "playing at being soldiers". [113]

Robert Procathren, the young poet who is to take Southman to London, arrives in the course of the old man's sour
yet delighted denunciation of society as a whore, which
begins the second act. Stella, determined to take the opportunity offered by his visit of escape from a debilitating existence, makes him promise to help her: but she believes that
events may have proceeded beyond "the point of deviation", so that no return is possible. Despite her warning,
Paul and Charles coarsely reject an appeal from Giles Aldus,
the rector sent as emissary from the village, for their assistance in face of the common danger from the soldiers: instead
they prepare to enlist their help in wreaking a long-desired
revenge against the village.

Suddenly, this fantasy world—in part self-created, in part
a product of the play's sustained logical self-sufficiency—
is at once shattered and intensified by the death of Stella,
shot by Procathren. The shooting is apparently a stupid
accident, caused by the poet's amateurish inspection of
Southman's lovingly shown-off but loaded rifle: and its
symbolic point is a demonstration of the artist's incapacity
as man of action, its ironic point the fulfilment of Stella's
prophecy. The awakening—the discovery of "the body with
the failing heart lying in the corridor"—proves less bearable
than the fantasy, and Southman retreats into the intensified
illusion of madness. Meanwhile, the soldiers arrive: but it is
Procathren who welcomes them as allies, determined now to
force events to their conclusion.

The instruments of this fantastic nemesis make their way
to the village, and when the last act begins the women of the
place, forming a mock-choric group, have taken shelter in
the house from the fire which has swept through their
homes. Here again the symbolic level of the action extends
precariously into the actual: for the blaze has been started by

Aldus, who, convinced by Procathren of the worthlessness of his declared faith, has burnt the books which, instead of being that faith's embodiment, have become its substitute. This fusion of levels threatens bathos, or at least to betray its own self-consciousness. In fact, it is again redeemed by the use of formal parody—here, the deployment of the local postman, the messenger of classical tragedy, as the bearer of the ill tidings from the village. Procathren and the soldiers return: they take out Charles, desultorily trying to complete his mural with the dead Stella as his model, together with the happily deluded Southman to their retributive executions. A little village girl dances to the trumpet that proclaims them hanged: her name is Stella.

Earlier, other coincidences in nomenclature have cropped up. Stella refers to her own unborn infant as the child Paul, [127] and, of course, Southman himself shares an anniversary with his namesake. But how far has Paul himself really lived out the "saintliness" attributed to him by Stella? [106–7] And which St Paul is he anyway: the apostolic martyr of Christian tradition, or merely the self-deceived life-hater thus psychologised by humanists, who has instilled into generations of believers an ugly fear of their own bodily desires?

He is, of course, both. Once, as he puts it, he was a real turtle, telling the home truths that earned him exile for his pains. But now he is the prophet turned-in upon himself, a lone voice which has cried so long in the wilderness that its sound has shrivelled into a senile whine. And his influence has surely soured the physical relationship between Stella and Charles. If Nicholas in *Conditions of Agreement* had been retarded at adolescence, Southman here is sinking back into the second childhood of old age—with its failing memory, its incontinence, and its infantile pleasures and plottings. And

just as Nicholas enmeshed a whole household in his petty
plans of revenge, so Southman has inveigled Charles and
tries to inveigle Procathren and the escaped soldiers into his
obsessed scheming against the villagers. But in the event
it is the soldiers who state their "conditions of agreement",
making terms with Procathren instead, and destroying the
homes of the villagers and the lives of Southman and
Charles.

The play's density of structure and its occasionally superfluous overtones of language do combine to blur the full
force of its apocalyptic vision. The failure is, however, one of
emphasis—of too much ornate overlay upon classically
straightforward outlines. Thus, since there is obviously
considerable significance in Whiting's choice of christian
names for his main characters, his use of heavily suggestive
surnames even for the lowliest of the villagers might easily
tempt one into a wild-goose-chase, if one wasn't aware that
he had admitted them to be chosen more or less at random.[15]
And fitting these villagers *physically* into the action, as well as
into Southman's imagined scheme of things, raises a lot of
questions which go half-answered.

Thus, Giles Aldus—carefully described in the cast list
not as the local rector but as "a recluse" [88]—is an intriguing but only partially rendered character. What does
Procathren say to him before he burns his books? What are
the reasons for his own choice of isolation? And why does he
keep both his mother and his "legendary" library from
contact with the world? [124] Of course all these touches
help to make up the play's distinctive texture: but what one
might be inclined to describe as the more wilful ones give it
opacity rather than helpful complexity.

A few early passages of awkward exposition apart, [92–3,
95–6] the play is, however, technically much tidier than

Conditions of Agreement. The movement of the piece towards its climax is conventional, but even the imposition of a "well-made" shape upon its essentially amorphous action gives an audience certain familiar bearings in unfamiliar territory. The first act sets the scene and establishes the ethical premises; the second puts these to a test which they fail, precipitating the crisis—and leaving the outsiders, Procathren and the soldiers, to resolve the action in the third. Some critics have claimed that this "shift of responsibility" in the last act—it is described in just these words by Procathren at the close of the second [147]—unbalances the play, and makes its resolution anti-climactic. But to the climax Whiting's sense of *relativistic* normality—or relativistic absurdity, if you like—is vital and redeeming. It is futile to play games of consequences with the play: considered in social or in legal terms, for example, the vacuum in which the action takes place (evidently a vacuum in the heart of the English countryside) must of course collapse inwards. But the isolation of the village and an acceptance of the *self-containment* of the actions which take place within it are—as in the remarkably similar case of John Arden's *Serjeant Musgrave's Dance*—the only demands the play makes for the suspension of its audience's disbelief. Once accepted, the self-containment saves the action from becoming unwieldy, and keeps it consistent and sequential within the closed circle of its worked-out retribution. In other words, the one absolute demand the play makes upon its spectators is for a willingness to penetrate sympathetically beyond the circumference of that circle.

Formally as well as thematically self-contained, the piece observes the three quasi-aristotelian unities even more closely than *Conditions of Agreement*. Indeed, the whole play has strong affinities with classical tragedy—with aeschylian tragedy especially, in its sense of resignation towards an inscrutable fate rather than in any attempt at rebellion against it. This impression is, of course, particularly strong at the opening of the third act, when the use of the village postman as the messenger reporting violent events offstage, and the village women's vicarious choric response, serve several purposes—not least important, of course, purely functional and descriptive ones. But this episode also permits a lessening of tension, and represents a lightening of dramatic touch after the immediate intensities of the first two acts, and in anticipation of the violence to follow—violence which, like the death of Stella and the fire, takes place in true classic fashion offstage. Thus the focus of the tragedy is at once extended and sharpened. The soldiers, too, become not only acceptable but integral to the action if conceived in these terms—for rationally, as Aldus remarks, their actions are inexplicable:

There seems to be no reason for their acts. They are madmen. I do not understand! I do not understand! [134]

But dramatically the soldiers are the Eumenides, the avenging furies, whose arrival after the crucial moment of the action—the moment of Stella's death—becomes not only appropriate but inevitable.

And, just as vague sympathy for suffering forms a singularly inadequate response to, say, *The Trojan Women*, Whiting makes it difficult for an audience's attention to be diverted into simply being sorry for his characters—instead (and this is the intention of the emotional distancing) the degree of their responsibility must be assessed. For if *Saint's Day* is about self-destruction, it is also about how far the individual is responsible for actions which bring self-destruction in their wake. The sense of emotional detachment is carefully maintained even in the case of the relatively unimportant character of Aldus. Thus, when the rector makes his vain appeal for help, Whiting specifies that he has "a marked impediment in his speech", and that by the end of the interview "Aldus has foundered upon his incoherence". And sure enough, in the play's Stratford East revival the clergyman's near-apoplectic condition was rendered with horrifying intensity. Yet the scene never approached melodrama, because of the distancing effect of the complex demands made on its audience—whose instinctive but sentimentalised sympathy for a man crumbling before their eyes was balanced by Southman's ironic but precise analysis of the rector's "self-conscious pathos". [137]

At one moment the supernumerary villagers are blamed, at the next excuses are made for them. "They hate us because they don't understand our isolation. They don't understand us and so they fear us. They fear us and so they hate us." [95] This is Stella's first explanation—an indictment of society-in-microcosm for despising what it cannot understand, just as society at large forced Southman into exile in revenge for his telling of unpalatable truths. But is even this responsibility too simply assigned? Later, Stella admits that the villagers have "cause for grievance and for hating us".

When Paul came here—when he withdrew from the world that attacked him—he chose the village to be his butt. . . . I remember the things he said about the village when I was a child—unforgivable, beastly and unprovoked. [113]

Society, like the village, and like Southman himself, has

been provoked in its own eyes, and has been the aggressor in the eyes of the attacked. There is nothing startling or original about any chain of cancelled-out recrimination such as this, except that here its mutually-destructive effects spiral with circular viciousness towards a retributive tragedy.

In a position curiously similar to Whiting's as a playwright, Southman and his family are members of an elite forced to win—in this case beg—their bread from an uncomprehending proletariat. Whiting was, however, sufficiently clear-sighted not to allow his characters the self-indulgence of their indigence. Both as a family unit and as individuals, therefore, the major characters, like the minor, repel sympathy even as they attract it—an intended ambivalence which marks out their personal tragedies as pitiable yet also contemptible. There is no clear-cut responsibility for the condition of dissociated reality in which these people have entrenched themselves: but if there is no simple attribution of guilt, neither is there of innocence. First, there is Southman's own complicity. In the past, as in the present, he has been poseur as well as prophet, and in Procathren's naïve description of his motives for imposing exile upon himself there is a suggestion that his sense of wounded dignity was uncomfortably akin to a fit of the sulks:

> You withdrew yourself from us, and with yourself your advice and guidance, to punish us for our treatment of you and your ideas. [121]

Now wilful withdrawal has atrophied into something approaching a persecution-complex, so that even the loyalty of John Winter becomes a matter for doubt and disputation. [102]

Secondly, there is Stella's complaisance—and a sort of

supine selfishness besides. She refuses either sympathy or assistance to her husband, a refusal typified—and the occasion is reminiscent of *Conditions of Agreement*—in her failure to assist Charles as he fell from the scaffolding supporting his canvas. "I called out for you as I fell—you didn't hear me." [99] Stella seldom hears calls for help. And then there is Charles's absorption in the old man's fantasy, which has enervated him as an artist. Once an infant prodigy, [123] he is now just an infant, joining in a game of soldiers that escalates during the action into reality.

And finally there is Procathren, whose first entrance interrupts Southman's mock-indictment of himself for the assault of that "well-known and much loved whore society", in that he did, "with malice and humour, reveal her for what she is, and not for what men wish her to be". [120] But the whore society from which the family chose to escape has merely been supplanted by the whore illusion: and Procathren's task is what was once Southman's—to lay bare and to expiate that illusion, which has for a time been comforting but is ultimately insidious. Simultaneously Procathren is to achieve the expiation of his own, humanistic illusion. In one sense, he is simply the conventional outsider of the well-made play—caught up in an action which his arrival unexpectedly sets under way, yet himself purified by it in his determination to "run towards the event . . . a thing I have never done before". [146] But in another sense he is the classical *deus ex machina*, an instrument of fatal and dispassionate logic. "The agency is human, not providential," says Paul, of Procathren's work with the pistol: [139] but Procathren might almost be a human agent of providence, and the timely arrival of his own agents, the escaped soldiers, is no less providential.

Yet even these soldiers, totally and anarchically irresponsible, acknowledge that responsibility needs to be vested in some authority. "If you want to order people like me around you've got to take the responsibility," Christian Melrose, their leader, therefore tells Procathren. [163] And, at every step, Procathren is pushed closer towards the fulfilment of his own role. It is Procathren who discovers the death of Southman's dog, the first hint of impending catastrophe: and he it is who kills Stella, though he is in no sense *morally* responsible for her death. But the existential responsibility for the action *has* been shifted to him. "Satisfied by the shift of responsibility, eh?" he asks Southman at the close of the second act, [147] and, accepting the shift, he duly completes the process of retribution as the play moves towards its close. No single person's responsibility is absolute, but neither is any individual completely innocent. The process is indeed, as Whiting suggested, one of fulfilled self-destruction.

Stella's death literally and metaphorically completes the picture. It is her dead body which serves as the model for the final figure in Charles's mural, and it is her death, though it precedes the final catastrophe, which points to the central fatalism of the play. Tautologically, the end-product of self-destruction is death: and yet, according to the play's metaphysic, death need not be a process of self-destruction. Stella states her belief that "the purpose of any memory, of any experience" is "to give foundation to the state of death".

Understand that whatever we do today in this house— this damned house—will provide some of the material for our existence in death and you understand my fear. No one who has lived as I have lived could be happy in death. It is impossible. [114–15]

And Procathren, stripped of his liberal optimism in a con-

frontation with his own innate violence—which anticipates
Bernard Sands's trauma in Angus Wilson's *Hemlock and
After*, just as it echoes, for example, the Elder's lamentation
for his loss of faith in Shaw's *Too True to be Good*—confesses
at the play's conclusion:

> Southman—I thought the power invested was for good.
> I believed we were here to do well by each other. It isn't
> so. We are here—all of us—to die. Nothing more than
> that. We live for that alone. You've known all along,
> haven't you? Why didn't you tell me—why did you have
> to teach me in such a dreadful way? For now—I have
> wasted my inheritance! All these years trying to learn how
> to live leaving myself such a little time to learn how to
> die. [164]

Learning how to die: there is certainly something aeschylian about this stripped-to-the-bone awareness. The language
has an entirely successful formality and yet, syntactically,
is casual and idiomatic. It's as if Whiting's intention here,
as in Stella's earlier speech (which is given climactic emphasis
at the end of the first act as Robert's is at the close of the
third), was to explicate his action by means of organic but
recognisably heightened statements—choric interludes, to
preserve the classical analogy. Certainly, motifs of decay and
death accumulate throughout the play—the dog, the trees
which once overshadowed the house but which are now
dead and must be felled, [103] even Stella's grey hairs, discovered by her much younger husband. [99] And in the
village there are no young men. [135]

In marked contrast to *Conditions of Agreement*, the play is
not about retarded childhoods but second childhoods—
although Robert, at the close of the second act, is reduced to

hurling ten-year-old abuse at Southman, and Southman, in turn, abandons playing at soldiers for playing with the little child who turns out to be his grand-daughter's name-sake. Obviously, in this action, and in this last coincidence of all, there is a hint of redemption: but it is no more than a hint. If the child Stella lives, the child Paul has died in his mother's womb.

There is no "unknown hand at the switch", waiting to effect the pauline "revelation by light", claims Procathren. "The way is from darkness to darkness to darkness." [164] Paul Southman has been the apostle of darkness. Robert Procathren has been his convert, and a family and a village his victims—victims of a mind more inscrutable and infinitely more potent, yet ultimately as erratic, careless and infantile in its actions as had been the practical-joking mentalities of Nicholas and Peter in the earlier play. There, threatened violence and vengeance petered out into inconsequence. Here, a climax is intended and achieved. Whiting, handling his material and his language with virtuosity and above all with tact, has kept emotions strong, but also strongly defined: and whereas the studied triviality of the events in *Conditions of Agreement* concentrated attention on the abstract issues they illustrated, here the enormity of the events reflects only the enormity of the human issues involved.

2

Festive Summer

A Penny for a Song

A PENNY FOR A SONG was written in 1949, and first staged,
a few months before *Saint's Day*, in March 1951. It is a play
very much of its period, and it was scarcely surprising that
what Ronald Hayman has aptly dubbed its "austerity
version",[16] prepared for the revival in 1962, should have
seemed so much less valuable and engaging a work. After all,
1951 was the year of the Festival of Britain, 1962 the year
of the Cuba Crisis; and although such hardy-annual tags
leave much truth untold about their respective times they
do suggest a pervasive mood, a tang in the air. If there is a
debt to be acknowledged to a person as well as to a period,
it is thus to Christopher Fry: though since his influence—
which is on the sensibility of the piece rather than its substance—is well assimilated, and not a cause of dissonance as
was Eliot's in *Saint's Day*, it is best mentioned briefly, noted
as another characteristic which "places" the play in the
early fifties, and forgotten. What matters here is that *A
Penny for a Song*, as Whiting has said and as one can readily
sense, "was written at a time of great personal happiness",
when "it seemed natural that such a feeling should be
expressed in a play".[17] Thus, to cloud the brilliance of what
was conceived as a summer daydream with hindsighted
glimpses of storms on the horizon was to make the action
untrue to itself, and it is with the earlier version of the play

—also the one preferred for the definitive edition of Whiting's work[18]—that I shall be dealing here.

The action is set in the garden of the west country home of Sir Timothy Bellboys at the time of the Napoleonic wars. Invasion is expected daily, and to guard against surprise attack the family's docile dogsbody Humpage scans the horizon from his treetop vantage-point, doubling as lookout for any conflagrations which might require the willing services of Sir Timothy's brother Lamprett, self-appointed fireman to the neighbourhood. Humpage, pervasively present, is a living symbol of the play's sense of stability. "There was a noise," as Pippin the maidservant remarks to him after a mildly earth-shattering explosion, "but if you're still there everything must be all right". [231]

"It is rarely necessary," wrote Whiting of *A Penny for a Song*, "to embroider the finer lunacies of the English at war."[19] Thus, Sir Timothy is planning to defeat Napoleon single-handed by the simple expedient of impersonating him, and telling the invading armies to return home in phrasebook French. Lamprett tends his fire-engine and awaits the call from Humpage. The blind Edward Sterne, whose abrupt arrival on the scene and more or less instant betrothal to Lamprett's daughter Dorcas takes nobody by surprise, is on his way to London to persuade the king to stop the war, [183] and his young companion and guide Jonathan is journeying to Bethlehem because nobody has the heart to tell him that Jesus is dead. [184] Some temporary confusion is caused when Sir Timothy fails to receive a warning from the commander of the local home guard that his Fencibles are about to hold an invasion exercise, since Sir Timothy mistakes this for the real thing and the Fencibles mistake Sir Timothy for Napoleon. But fortunately Lamprett is vigilant in extinguishing the warning beacons as soon as

they are lit, so little damage is done before the mistake is
discovered and the erstwhile combatants adjourn to discuss
the niceties of cow-breeding and cricket.

The play is vividly, sometimes startlingly, theatrical. The
original production was, with utter appropriateness, designed by Rowland Emett—the cartoonist, and creator of the
Emett Railway in the Festival Pleasure Gardens. Those
gardens were full of similar, zanily mechanised or tortuously
rustic devices, like the Guinness Clock and the Tree Walk,
and these signs of their times are also suggestive of the visual
impression the play itself makes. Huge, heath-robinsonish
jokes abound. There is the rise and fall of Sir Timothy in a
requisitioned circus balloon. There is the appearance of
Hester in the full armorial regalia of the East Anglian
Amazon Corps she is about to join as a non-commissioned
officer. [239] And, of course, there is Lamprett's elaborate
firefighting equipment, including, of all things, a complicated
firework for blowing up conflagrations, [200] not to mention
the vintage engine itself—which makes a brief personal
appearance at the beginning of the second act for no other
reason than to be shown off. [212–13] Even the house itself
—its practical doll's house doors and windows forever
opening and shutting to display small housekeeping activities
within—becomes part of this toytown world, overflowing
with fancy-dressed inhabitants.

As for these inhabitants, their childlike delight in complicated apparatus is combined with a childlike acceptance of
the unexpected at its face value. Surprise guests like Hallam
Matthews, a sardonic philosopher in retreat from urban
bustle, are unquestioningly found a room. Total strangers
like Edward Sterne are given food and hospitality. And
unknown little boys like Jonathan are good-naturedly seized
on sight for fire-engine servicing. [184] Even the formidable-

looking Hester only bullies so as not to belie her appearance. After all, if a cannon-ball comes bounding through one's garden gate, the sensible thing to do is to shut the gate: [216] just another instance of what Dorcas soon afterwards describes as that very English refusal to admit that something has happened, and determination to carry on as if nothing ever could. [217] Humpage "remains at his post", [212] and the characters who cluster around his tree come and go in constantly varying combinations, from philosophical two-somes to family gatherings—all contributing, of course, to the impression of life and movement, of exits and entrances, the orchestration of so many cuckoo-clocks.

It's difficult to try to sum up the play's scenic quality or the infinite capacity of its characters for assimilating sur-prises without making it seem merely whimsical—and out-datedly whimsical at that. But it is precisely the integration of characters and setting which avoids whimsy: and, as in all Whiting's plays, this setting is carefully described, and emerges out of the action instead of being daubed on later as an afterthought. Thus, dissimilar though the country-garden setting of *A Penny for a Song* may be in tonal contrasts and summery textures from the overcast interiors of *Conditions of Agreement* and *Saint's Day*, it shares with them a stressed incongruity—which here focuses on Humpage, pervasive in his tree and surrounded by all his impedimenta of fire alarms, spy-glasses and invasion signals. Scenically, at least, it's as if the piece were a parodistic gloss upon the earlier works: and thematically, too, there are conscious or un-conscious echoes, which bounce back rounded and more optimistic across that "period of personal happiness" during which the play was conceived—a period which, as far as its reflection in Whiting's creative work was concerned, was to be unique.

Beneath the pleasurably nonchalant surface of the action, the inner philosophical core of the play thus concerns the problems and pains involved in accepting illusion—the problem, in particular, of preserving happiness and a sense of purpose at the expense of self-deception. Given the tragic twist, as in *Saint's Day*, self-deception could proceed only towards self-destruction, for there it involved the abdication of responsibility. Here, it is the acceptance, joyfully, of what is conceived to *be* responsibility that redeems the deception: and instead of a tragic shadow a shaft of clear, comedic daylight falls between the intention and the act.

"We find reality unbearable," as Edward Sterne puts it, "the infrangible burden to carry: self-knowledge. And so we escape, childlike, into the illusion. We clown and posture, but not to amuse others—no—to comfort ourselves. The laughter is incidental to the tragic spectacle of each man attempting to hide his intolerable self." But "what we call the illusion—you and I—which is the laughter and the happiness and the sudden flowering of love, perhaps that is the reality". [219] It is, then, purposefulness that sanctifies illusion, even if the purpose, too, is illusory.

Hallam thus dispels Edward's hopes of peacemaking, but still he must journey to London to see a mad king: for him "there is no escape . . . only a little purpose". [242] Perhaps (because of his illusion rather than in spite of it, as Hallam admits) he will succeed. [221] Timothy remarks of his impersonation scheme: "I may fail—but what of that. It is what we attempt that matters." [196] And Lamprett explains to Hallam, who can't help feeling that *he* ought to be doing the explaining: "Our destination is unimportant. We journey forward only to discover the reason for our travelling." [243]

In an evidently more bitter mood, Whiting excised most of this philosophical gloss when revising the play, and substituted a pragmatic, proselytising radical for the easier-going Edward of the original version.[20] Yet the soldierly sourness did not blend well, whereas the admitted naïvety of the text as it stood had provoked an audience to soul-searching even as it caught one eyebrow raised in deprecatory cynicism. Once the cynicism was written in, the naïvety no longer acted as its own corrective. "All it states," Whiting has claimed for his original work, "in very simple terms, is the idea of Christian charity."[21] And in this original, the charity illuminates and even, in its sheer ebullience, instructs—as a lesson in "enjoying this charming occupation known as life". [178]

If there is anything contentious about Whiting's declaration of his theme, it lies in the assumption that it is possible at all adequately to treat Christian charity "in very simple terms": but in the event, although the play captures the *innocence* of its situation and its characters, it does not do so by simplifying them. For example: one reason why the radical Edward Sterne was so much less interesting than the blind wayfarer was that he merely doubled a debunking role already filled by another character—that refugee from the city who feels it his duty to keep up with the latest heresies of Mr Wordsworth, but who spends a fair portion of his time snoozing in an alcove, Hallam Matthews.

Although Hallam is no innocent, he, too, is charitable: he prods only gently and with a certain awe the innocence of others. Yet he does not so much practise Christian charity as, mildly disconcerted, find himself on its receiving end. And he recognises that, among all the gentle people in whose household he finds himself, Dorcas is most in danger of stumbling against a sudden, sharp outcrop of reality. He begs her not to make too many demands upon those with whom she would share her dawning adulthood:

What an inquisitive child you are! You must learn to accept things—attitudes—especially if you're going to be in love. More important then than at any other time: for love itself is only a delicious pose to gain for ourselves the comfort we all so deeply need. [218–19]

And for Jonathan, too, Hallam has a warning against over-hasty growing-up:

Were someone to overlook us now they would take it that Innocence conversed with Experience. In that latter part what can I say to you? I feel I should say something, don't you? The situation requires it. Very well, then: retain the defensive weapons of your childhood always, my dear. They are invaluable, these delights and amusements. [221]

Hallam here combines that detachment of so many of Whiting's characters towards themselves with an empathy towards others that is one of the less bitter fruits of experience. He is an audience's rather than an author's mouthpiece: and like him, the members of an audience are nudged by his experience a little closer towards doing as they would be done by.

With one exception, the remaining characters are humorous—one would add, in the jonsonian sense, if it were not that their ruling inclinations are so good-natured as to defy their own best attempts to bring destruction upon their heads. As in *Conditions of Agreement*, the characters thus embody an abstraction—but that abstraction is Christian charity, and so whereas Nicholas and Peter were merely childish, they are childlike. The one exception is Dorcas, for whom the play is itself a kind of lesson in growing up, and

for whose entertainment the world is expressly designed.
As that compulsive verbaliser, Hallam, puts it:

> You, in your youth, regard us as your clowns, do you not?
> The world, spinning about the centre of your untouched
> heart, somersaults for your amusement. . . . But you
> must remember that there are some days when the clowns
> must sit together in the sun and talk of clownish things.
> Even if they sit together for no other reason than to think
> up new ways of distracting you. [197]

To enjoy clowning—and one can't help recalling A.G.'s
wife in *Conditions of Agreement*, the first of so many circus-
lovers in Whiting's work—one needs to be childlike. Yet
Dorcas's age of seventeen, as it occurs to Hester at the
beginning of the play, "is the time to put off your childish
ways". [178] This Dorcas dutifully endeavours to do in her
conversations—and her falling in love—with Edward
Sterne:

> HESTER: Ah, Dorcas, I never seem to be able to find you.
> What have you been doing?
> DORCAS: Putting off childish ways.
> HESTER: I see. [205]

Here is the play in a nutshell—its tone of voice, its style of
humour, and one of its main themes. Hester accepts Dorcas's
explanation without so much as a raised eyebrow. That Dorcas
makes it at all is part and parcel of the play's internal logic,
and its wry habit of turning that logic back upon itself.
And that it is, in a sense, the *correct* explanation is borne out
by Whiting's earlier concern with the nature of innocence
and experience: here, the play, as plaything for Dorcas,

instructs her in remaining childlike while outgrowing what is merely childish.

Both *Conditions of Agreement* and *Saint's Day* were about the over-simplified, undeviating solutions adopted by tortuously complicated characters—intentionally to resolve, but in effect to consolidate, their tendencies towards self-destruction. *A Penny for a Song* is, in contrast, about very simple people adopting the most tortuous solutions they can devise, in pursuit of illusory goals. But because they are sought for an unselfish end, the illusions themselves are redeemed.

Here, as in *Saint's Day*, the local rector is to be found visiting the scene of the action, and giving—as John Winter did in the earlier play—a report on the situation "in a commendable manner". [224] Here, too, the "military" situation precipitates a fire: but in *A Penny for a Song* the fire is put out harmlessly, and, for the firefighters, most satisfyingly. Whether such faint echoes are in deliberate parody of the earlier play is scarcely important: what is interesting is how intention and attitude can thus transform the threatening into the promising, the storm of *Saint's Day* into the sunshine of *A Penny for a Song*. For Whiting, however, the sunny interval was to be brief. His next play was also to be about the efficacy of a life-lie: but in *Marching Song* the slender thread giving meaning and purpose to life was to be as casually snapped as it had been carefully woven.

3

Above the Battle

Marching Song and *The Gates of Summer*

WHITING'S NEXT PLAY took its title from one of Yeats's *Marching Songs*—a wry statement of the soldier's need for a cause and for a commander, even if the cause is empty and the commander fallible. It poses the question:

What if there's nothing up there at the top?
Where are the captains that govern mankind?[22]

And Whiting explores the consequences upon one man of loss of faith—alike in his cause, and in the illusion he has nurtured in its place.

Whiting himself believed that *Marching Song*—written in 1951-2, and staged briefly at the St Martin's Theatre in 1954—was the "most important" of his early plays,

both in content and structure. It has a single and un-deviating line in story and treatment which is inclined to make it forbidding in performance. The play is built around the figure of Forster, the soldier. There are no sub-plots, and within the action of the play no character has any activity outside the relation with Forster. My intention was to strip from the play everything unimportant to the theme, both in speech and action. This, of course,

makes for a deliberate formality of pattern and an
austerity of movement. Very little happens. It is an anti-
theatrical play.[23]

What does happen, briefly, is this. Rupert Forster has been a
prisoner of war in the hands of his country's conquerors for
seven years. The occupation over, and a "democratic"
regime installed in office, Forster is released: and as the
action of *Marching Song* opens, he has just returned to the
home of his former mistress, Catherine de Troyes, set "on
the heights above a capital city in Europe". [257] In Forster's
absence, Catherine has gathered about her a strange trio of
platonic companions—Harry Lancaster, an American film
producer whose little skill in his craft has long since dis-
appeared; Matthew Sangosse, a physician; and Father
Anselm, a priest. All are now seemingly superfluous to her
needs: but Rupert's return threatens to be, all too literally,
short lived. For Cadmus, the nation's new chancellor,
arrives, to warn him that unless he is prepared to take his
own life he will be brought to a fresh trial—this time by his
fellow-countrymen, as a convenient scapegoat for defeat, his
inexplicable behaviour in halting a successful wartime
advance sufficient excuse for his being singled out.

Rupert no longer loves Catherine, who only imagines
herself in love with a seven-year-old memory, and he faces
the prospect of suicide stoically. But he meets Dido Morgen,
a young city girl Harry has picked up with a vague promise
of fitting her into a new film: and in a sequence of conversations with her—the two minds meeting strangely across
generations separated by the experience of war—Rupert
finds reason enough to fight for his life. Catherine, more
concerned that Rupert should cling to his life than that she
should cling to a lost lover, therefore persuades Dido to

c

remain. Rupert is apparently now determined to stand trial: but as his time for decision expires with the dawn of a second day—the action of the play spanning a mere thirty-six hours in all—Cadmus withdraws the guard, and he takes the opportunity to kill himself. It is now Catherine who needs Dido's help, and this, not really knowing how or why, she reluctantly agrees to give.

The formal discipline noted by Whiting contributes to the explicitness with which *Marching Song* comes across in production, although it also makes this in some ways the least rewarding of Whiting's plays. In intention one feels that its formality is more anti-melodramatic than (at least in the sense in which Whiting was using the term) anti-theatrical: and the ability to strike an appropriately spare style—refining emotions without refining them out of existence—will determine the play's fate in production. The earlier richness of language is dissipated, allusive overtones are rigorously pruned, and the result is the clipped precision of, for example, this potted-autobiography of Dido's:

> People like me don't think about the future. We don't matter you see. If we survive—that's good. If we go out —well, there's not much harm done. Mind, if somebody tries to put us out before we think it's time, we fight. What for? Just to stay alive, to see one more day end, have one more hot bath, be made love to once more, hear one more tune we've heard before and got fond of. This is apt to make us a nuisance about the place, but you people are getting better at making bigger gadgets to end all that. [285]

This is closer to the over-careful colloquialism of a Rattigan than to Eliot or Fry. The language is still loaded with slightly stilted self-analysis, but the author's own identification with his character is less certain—and there is, too, an unusual though muted note of didacticism. Whiting claimed that the theme of *Marching Song*, was, like that of *Saint's Day*, self-destruction:[24] and although the fatalism of the earlier play is here modified by the faint hope that Dido can perhaps teach Catherine to live without the kind of self-diminishing illusion which has destroyed her lover, there is something schematic about the intention as there is about the action.

The problem, strangely, is that here the characters are not *sufficiently* abstract. "Everything unimportant to the theme" has *not* been stripped away: the attempt has been made, true enough, so that the bones of the plotting tend to protrude, but there are awkward, human edges to the characters which make them less than congruent to the kind of action in which they're caught up. "Mr. Whiting," commented the critic of *The Times*, "appears more interested in ideas than in people."[25] So he often was, of course: but he usually showed more skill in giving abstraction a human face. Here, those characters who succeed best in embodying an abstract idea are the most satisfactory—but in the small-time way of Cadmus, who represents the necessities of political power, or of Harry, the failed and insufficient liberal humanist. It is the large-scale, and potentially most interesting characters, Dido and Rupert, who beg the most questions, and step furthest outside the play's "deliberate formality of pattern".

This is certainly Whiting's most ibsenesque play. Not only is it about the efficacy of a life-lie, but its actors have a habit of asserting their own symbolism—as Harry does for instance, burning his hands while destroying the single remaining print of his film, and, with it, his past. Even the three levels of the setting are laden with an obtrusive visual symbolism—the staircases leading up and down from the majestic but purgatorial room in which the entire action takes place doing service as referents for heaven and hell. [275, 316] And the effects gained are decisively too cheap at the price. The set of *Marching Song* is, indeed, much less integral to its action than is that of *Saint's Day*. It, too, is distinctive and unique: "a shell caught within a web of glass and steel", which "transcends the mere purpose of a dwelling place". It gives "an impression of delicacy, almost fragility", yet is "a fortress in strength and position". [257] And the place is set apart—isolated from contagion—from "that stinking city" [264] whence corrupt politicians and Harry's stragglers alike come. But why is this so important? For the action that has shaped the action, as it were, has taken place not here, but in Rupert's prison camp in the country, and in the streets and bars of Dido's city.

The room fits only Catherine—though her it fits like a glove, at once protective and isolating. Yet, in spite of the shift in the play's focus towards her in its final moments, Catherine remains a shadowy, almost peripheral figure. During the seven years of Rupert's imprisonment she has lived in self-imposed exile, [270] but neither the enormity nor the anguish of her love is truly manifest; and even her sacrifice in accepting that Rupert's best hope of fulfilment now lies with Dido seems a muffled, almost perfunctory gesture. [289] It's as if her passion has been scaled down to fit an almost over-civilised play, in which suicide and a rigged trial for treason are matters for calm debate between an avowed opportunist and the victim of his politics of expediency.

The play's abstraction, then, is its saving grace as it is its weakness. The illusion-reality opposition is the theme which is most fully explored, its scrupulously balanced dialectic represented by Cadmus and Dido—the one defending and the other damning the efficacy of a life-lie. True, Cadmus's version of pseudo-democracy contains its own implicit indictment, in that he consciously nourishes, for political ends, his country's capacity for self-deception. "The way to prevent revolt is to stop men living in the present time," he believes, and feeds his people a diet of pap and nostalgia. A little taken aback by Dido, he asks:

Are there many like that, I wonder? Is it a volcano I'm sitting on and not, as I'd supposed, a dung-hill? [298]

But he is not seriously concerned with the problem: its imagery interests him more than its solution. What Cadmus can argue convincingly enough is the practical necessity for a political system based on the stoking of the dunghill.

Now Whiting himself shared Cadmus's contempt for democracy—not because it could be so easily manipulated, but because, as he saw it, the concept was just another means of papering over one's evasions of individual responsibility. And in this sense, even Dido's acceptance of reality —which is essentially an acceptance of the immediacy of life—is an evasion. Dido is a strikingly modern character: she has something of the innocent experience of Ivich in Sartre's *Age of Reason* about her, anticipating, and almost dignifying, the heretical existentialism of living for kicks. She had believed that Forster was dead, [260] as A.G. had thought Peter Bembo was dead in *Conditions of Agreement*: and she shares something of Patience's horror in that play of dwelling or relying upon the past for present consolation. Thus, of her own name—and this is a unique instance of a Whiting character drawing attention to an oddity in nomenclature—she remarks:

Please don't laugh. Blame my father. He was an archaeologist. Always grubbing in the past. Disgusting occupation.
[281]

It's notable, by the way, how easily Dido's speech manner-
isms could be adapted into those of a stock aristocratic lady
of Edwardian vintage: the individual has been fitted to the
idiom, it seems, and not vice-versa.

Anyway, one senses that Whiting was never really at
home with Dido—feeling very strongly *what* she was, but
less surely how her individuality could best be verbalised:

I don't know anything. All right? I'm the girl you see on
the edge of the crowd at a street accident. It's got nothing
to do with me. I just happened to be there. I don't want
to be a witness. All right? [297]

All right as far as the image fits Dido: but precisely because
it *does* fit her, it is too well-considered for her ever to have
said it. "Cleanliness before wantonness, you know," Whiting
even makes her epigrammatise at one point, [258] as if,
having denied himself the kind of language in which he used
to luxuriate, he felt he ought to do his best at raising a more
seemly titter from the stalls: there's a lot of this kind of thing
at the beginning of the play, from Harry as well as from
Dido.

Nevertheless, as a character Dido does exert an extraordinary fascination. She is a generation in embryo, and she
seems constantly on the verge of making great discoveries
about herself and her motives. "Quite soon now the day will
come," says Catherine, "when you'll have to admit that the
anger and despair you feel is not because of other people.
It is for them." [304] Catherine need not necessarily be

right about this: but she, like the audience, senses the imminence of the cast-off chrysalis.

Caught between Cadmus and Dido is Rupert Forster: for him, acceptance of the philosophy of the politician means death, commitment to the instinctive demands of the girl means life. The choice may or may not be symbolic: but it is quite certainly literal. However, Forster's physical death is of small moment—certainly of no such purport as Stella's, which had marked the turning-point of *Saint's Day*. Here, rather, the crucial moment—the "point of deviation" —has occurred long before the play begins. It is re-lived in Forster's long description [294–5] of his traumatic confrontation with a child's death, for which he was personally responsible. Conceiving himself a sort of nietzschian superman—destined to "pursue a triumph of arms", since "by that I believed I could become myself, the man I was intended to be" [294]—the young Forster had sought what he conceived to be self-fulfilment, at whatever cost to others. And the death of an obstructive urchin was militarily a necessity, therefore a necessity for his own advancement. But in the aftermath of its commission he "became human", and able to perceive not merely a cause, but the individual he had murdered. [314]

The action on stage is thus strictly speaking anti-climactic, a gradual falling-away towards Forster's final acceptance of his responsibility in death: and this redemption of past guilt has no such ironic overtones as are felt in *Saint's Day*, because Forster's personal guilt has been admitted, confronted, and expiated. The process is remorseless—and one does begin to feel as the play's focus centres, albeit belatedly, upon Rupert, that "single and undeviating line in story and treatment" which Whiting had intended. In the process Rupert is stripped of every illusion with which he has tried to make existence bearable. Even his refusal to make prison-life a little more tolerable for himself by the exercise of imagination and the play of memory is shown to have been a futile demonstration of independence. "It could have been any of my particular heavens or hells," he claims. "I chose that the room should be a brick and steel cell in a prison camp in the mountains." [270–1] He believed he had become human by recognising humanity, and only needed to keep the line of contact open in prison by recognising it in another—as it happened, in the song of a goat-herd, audible every morning from his cell. "I ended by understanding that you can't shut out the human voice—especially when it's expressing itself in an act of faith." [300] But the "act of faith" is revealed (quite casually, by the young guard Cadmus has set over Rupert) to have been an obscenity: "the goat-herd's expression of love—to his goats. The songs don't make sense". [312]

Earlier, Rupert has accused Harry Lancaster of mistaking his motives in his wish for Dido's company:

Lancaster has a liberal mind. To him no man is entirely evil. Not even me. And so he is compelled to mistake my gestures of defiance for signals of distress. [301]

There is a complex irony here. Identifying with Lancaster's conventional view of himself as a human monster, he has Harry "make allowances" for what seems, after all, a human failing—sexual desire. But it is, indeed, very much open to doubt whether Forster's small dependences—on the goat-herd's song, as on Dido's company—are gestures of defiance or distress. And the songs, at least, are metamorphosed from one to the other with vertiginous suddenness. It is soon after learning the truth about them that Rupert commits suicide

—as Cadmus, a public announcement to that effect ordered in advance, had always known he would.

In effect, this anticipation on Cadmus's part begs many questions. What *does* determine Rupert to commit suicide? If Cadmus is right, there was never any doubt, and much of the action becomes—according to Whiting's own statement that he "stripped away from the play everything unimportant to the theme"—dramatically irrelevant. If Cadmus is wrong, and there has been a real conflict, the public-address announcement is stagey at a very delicate moment of the action. This is symptomatic of a whole area—the party-political, as it were—in which Whiting's thematic ruthlessness skirts too many related issues. Cadmus's explanation of why it is necessary to bring Forster to trial is more or less instantly accepted by all the characters: yet the allegation that an opposition party which Cadmus himself derides as "liberal" should be the instigators of a demand for a scapegoat on whom to blame defeat in an evidently most illiberal and nationalistic war seems mildly improbable. And Cadmus's own wish to avoid the trial, and thus his reason for giving Rupert the opportunity of committing suicide, seems equally superficial in its certainty that, once this episode of an unsavoury period is resurrected, the mud "will stick to every man, woman, and child of this nation". [279] Indeed, far from the play having no "private parts", as Whiting once claimed, it is its failure to fuse its "public" action with the dominant (though not overtly sexual) personal level that makes these trivial flaws stick in the throat.

It's a pity that Whiting was anything like as explicit: in *Saint's Day* one is able to accept far greater improbabilities without a qualm. But the ostensible naturalism of the action here, and the pruning away of such thematic embellishments as concealed multitudinous sins of contextual omission in *Saint's Day*, directs attention to the defects. The play is not sufficiently dense to be self-sufficient in locale, or in rationale. And this weakness in sheer credibility combines with an uncertainty of emphasis—the early interest in Catherine only shifting towards Rupert after nearly an act of exposition and philosophising, and returning climactically to her, yet insufficiently sustained either by the substance of her role or by its supposed implication in Rupert's—to make the play the weakest in construction, for all that it's also the most tightly-knit, Whiting wrote.

Just as this is his most ibsenesque play, it is, however, often able to transcend its faults just as Ibsen transcends his symbolism. In particular, it is a whole lot more complex than Whiting suggested: the pruning process was evidently far from efficient. Two of the three friends who have helped Catherine through the nine years of Rupert's absence, first at war and subsequently in prison, are little more than ciphers: thus, in function, Sangosse the physician and Anselm the priest are almost interchangeable, and nothing of the personal qualities, let alone the dormant professional skills, which first attracted them to Catherine comes across when they do wander in, as if from some other play. But Harry Lancaster bulks larger both in the quantity and the quality of his contribution—which is far from being confined to his relationship with Forster. Indeed, this relationship consists mainly in their getting on each other's nerves, the most interesting feature of their antagonism being a subtle hint of sexual tension and jealousy, confusedly over both Catherine and Dido.

As an individual, though, Harry has more than a touch of the Willy Lomans, and he acts out a small, unconsummated tragedy of his own—a modern tragedy of self-deception, in effective counterpoint to Rupert's tragedy of over-developed self-awareness. "Twenty years ago I made the picture of my youth," he boasts to Dido: now he's going to make what "the magazines'll call the film of my maturity". But Harry probably knows as surely as does Catherine that the film will never be made: so he keeps the one remaining copy of his long-forgotten movie "against the dead days". [259] Shown for the amusement of the company, it proves to be —the judgement is Dido's—just another "damned bad film". [284] And Harry burns it in a fit of drunken self-pity. Like Stella in *Saint's Day*, he has been let down by those memories of the past which should be stored up in anticipation of death—the dead days, indeed. Self-proclaiming himself one of "us little people", [302] Harry represents and speaks for the mass which is out for Forster's blood: yet he is neither of the dunghill nor the volcano, merely a man histrionic in his sense of his own pathos, and pathetic in his fear of approaching death.

Harry, not realising the whole truth about Rupert's dilemma, but sure at least that the returned lover no longer feels much for his mistress, and is not trying to conceal the fact, implores him to "pretend for a while . . . that everything is just as it has been". [284] He is a firm believer in the life-lie as a prop for himself, too, commenting on Dido's attempt at an apology for falling asleep during his film:

The difficulty with you, sweetheart—and with him—is that you're honest about yourself. I'm sorry, but I've lost the talent for doing that sort of thing. [284]

This is true enough: and if Cadmus advocates the illusion which vitiates, at least Harry proposes the illusion that comforts.

What, then—to borrow Ronald Hayman's neat phraseology—is the moral difference between a life-lie and a life-line?[26] Rupert charges Harry with distorting the world around him to satisfy his own longing: but Catherine points out that this is at least less dangerous than "trying to destroy it to satisfy your ambition." [310] And Whiting himself remarked, with evident distaste, that the only character in the play "who comes towards any reasonable sort of humanity, is a fool like Lancaster. The girl is terribly cold."[27] Yes: for Dido's "honesty" about herself is prompted by the sheer instinctive easiness of concealing nothing—whilst Rupert's self-awareness has already proved to be a detour towards deception.

Catherine's exile has been in memory of a man who changed, abruptly and for the better, seven years before, and who can no longer love her: and although she believes Dido can teach her "to try to live again", [321] Dido herself isn't sure that this can be taught—and her decision to try is against Rupert's farewell advice to escape, rather than to get "caught in the memory of the past day". [318] If the play has any answer to the problems it poses about illusion and personal responsibility, it is only that, although there are plenty of false solutions, there is no demonstrably right one. "I suffer very much," Whiting once remarked, "from being able to see both sides of the question."[28]

This is the import of the message Rupert asks Dido to give to the young guard to whom he has told his story, and from whom he has learnt the truth about the goat-herd's songs. "Tell him," he says, "he's mistaken if he thinks he has learnt or will learn anything from my behaviour. I faced the same problems over the same ground as that man." And, indicating an antique helmet worn by a dead soldier in a battle long ago, he goes on to emphasise that Hurst will face the same problems in the future. "They are unchanging but the time and place of decision is personal." [318] These are almost Rupert's last words in the play—which is "about" not the right choice or the wrong choice, but the act of choosing. Whether the choice nudges one towards a greater reality, or sustains one in the uncertain security of illusion, will depend not on some immutable moral propriety but on circumstances. Which is—to return to the play's ibsenesque quality —very much what Ibsen was saying in *The Wild Duck*.

In spite of the failures of communication—with his audience rather than with his characters—one gets the feeling that *Marching Song* was the first of Whiting's serious plays to be written with an eventual performance in a theatre in the forefront of his mind. *Conditions of Agreement* and *Saint's Day* are instinctively theatrical, whereas *Marching Song* is full of scrupulously craftsmanlike touches. The varying modes of speech—from Dido's sometimes slightly precious patter and Harry's slurred pomposities to Cadmus's suave, studied periods—help to individualise the characters more strongly. And Rupert, Dido, and even Harry are more "real"—though not necessarily better or worse for it—than any of their predecessors. Variations in tone, and the carefully timed entrances of Cadmus and of Catherine's various hangers-on, keep the more philosophical dialogue from dragging, whilst Rupert's long confessional speech is in exactly the right place, almost but not quite at the end of the middle act.

Whether or not Rupert's delayed entrance makes up in suspense-building what it muffs in the way of emphasis is more open to question. But what is truly remarkable is how Whiting does succeed in keeping the melodrama—constantly simmering just below the surface—from openly erupting. The greater emotional intensity of *Saint's Day* finds continuous release in images and in acts of violence: but the violence of

Marching Song is once removed, and its delayed catharsis tends to build up tension rather than release it. To say that the dialectic demands made by the play successfully prevent it from shifting into melodramatic gear is not to imply, however, that they are positively helpful in keeping the arguments clearly sustained and the emotions sharply etched. If one doesn't actually topple over the brink into melodrama, one is seldom far enough from the edge to be able to forget the danger.

Maybe what is unbalanced about *Marching Song* is its attempt to explore an ibsenesque theme in a chekhovian manner. More aptly, in Whiting's next work, *The Gates of Summer*, a brooding locale and a bitter tragi-comic mood combined to create the first play in which he explicitly concerned himself with that peculiarly chekhovian problem —the problem of simply passing the time. It's worth recalling that towards the end of *Marching Song*, but before Dido agrees after all to remain, Catherine has been contemplating with Harry just this prospect of a leftover life to kill:

How shall we spend the time? All the time that's left. What shall we do with it? This fortune to be rid of. Shall we be charitable? Give me your part and I'll give you mine. But we have equal portions which makes it absurd. We shall end up where we began with no more and no less. There'll be no loss, no gain, but it will pass the time— the time we have to spend—it will pass the time, this give and take—it will pass the time. [322-3]

Those lines from *Marching Song* were written in 1951–52. Within three years another play, destined to dominate the drama of its generation, had been staged, which was to reflect both verbally and spiritually this impression of life as a *longueur* to be alleviated as best each individual might manage:

VLADIMIR: That passed the time.
ESTRAGON: It would have passed in any case.
VLADIMIR: Yes, but not so rapidly.
Pause.

This, of course, is Vladimir and Estragon commenting on their first visit from Pozzo and Lucky in Beckett's *Waiting for Godot*.[29] But Catherine's variation on the theme of boredom is, appropriately, a sharper foretaste to *The Gates of Summer*—for its characters, like those of *Marching Song*, are weighed down by wealth as well as by lethargy. Besides, Whiting was never a great formal innovator, so one would not expect him to have conjured up some quasi-beckettian universe of his own. He preferred to explore the bleakness of existence by slightly warping a more recognisable, even mundane, reality, so that its absurdity is that of a brobdingnagian pimple—gross, but certainly in correct proportion.

Whiting's examination of an outbreak of human acne in *The Gates of Summer*—written in 1953–54 and staged on tour in 1956—is too microscopic to be easily synopsised. But in the event its surface action is less important than that of any of the earlier plays. Like *Conditions of Agreement*, the play opens—in this case just before the First World War—as a lover returns to visit his former, now ageing mistress. The lover is John Hogarth, civilised debauchee in flight from the "baying of the newspapers" after his latest adultery, [17] and the mistress is Sophie Faramond—long since respectably married to the archaeologist Selwyn Faramond, exiled on her husband's endless expeditions, and at present living in a country house a little way from Athens. Nearby, Selwyn digs hopefully and doesn't get much nearer arriving, whilst Henry Bevis potters about wondering how to make himself better liked and sending weekly reports to *The Times* on the progress of the dig. Sophie's beautiful stepdaughter Caroline Traherne licks, not without a certain relish, the wounds of an early, disastrous marriage. And Sophie herself dictates her memoirs to her landlord-cum-secretary Christos, who rewrites them in his own image.

As the action begins, and as Sophie remarks in the first words in the play, spoken to Christos, "the man we have been trying to create is coming up the hill". [5] The mythic John Hogarth who has figured so prominently in Sophie's manuscript is to be tested against the ten-years-older reality, just as Catherine's memory of Rupert Forster was to clash with the returned prisoner in *Marching Song*. But whereas the clash in that previous play sparked a tragic tension, here it produces a situation bordering on farce. If *A Penny for a Song* was a well-tempered treatment of that illusion-reality opposition which had been more grotesquely resolved in *Saint's Day*, then *The Gates of Summer* is a kind of sardonic afterthought to *Marching Song*—the tests against which political action was there measured now applied to the practical joking of *Conditions of Agreement*.

Sophie, like Emily in *Conditions of Agreement*, begins by up-staging everybody during the first-act exposition, and then fades into the background, whilst Hogarth, like Charles in *Saint's Day*, has been intoxicated by "the rallying cries of manifestos and a mad old man". [12] He is in Athens to await the arrival of this "mad old man"—his political mentor and financial debtor Prince Basilios—and the call to revolutionary battle in the north. Although Hogarth has decided to give up women in Basilios's cause, he gets distracted (almost out of habit) by the beautiful Caroline, who is equally distracted by him. He lets himself make love to her, but refuses to give up his plans for the girl's sake: and so, if she can't beat Hogarth in life, Caroline prefers to join him in death, and tries to effect the suicide and the sacrifice simultaneously by adding the juices of a potent local herb to their farewell drink. In the eight hours between discovering he has been poisoned and the likely time of the herb's taking effect, Hogarth, agonising over his imminent demise, is interrupted by a breakthrough in the excavations: but instead of the sacred place of worship Selwyn had vaguely hoped to find, there is uncovered only a temple of profanity. Across the millennia, the obscene graffiti of the ancient world mock the erotic shufflings of the modern, as the goat-herd's bestial song had mocked Rupert Forster.

Whereas Rupert's poison was highly effective, however, Caroline's turns out to be a case of mistaken identity. "Man's Friend", the locals call the herb: and a misunder-standing of the ironic name has led Caroline to dope the wine with nothing worse or less apt than a reputed aphro-disiac. No sooner is Hogarth adjusted to the idea of a future again than his plans are upset a second time by the arrival of Basilios, who has blewed the money Hogarth gave him—his entire, now unwanted fortune—on a charity garden-party to which only his mistress turned up. Selwyn, his mission accomplished, drags Sophie off to pastures old; and the best Hogarth can do is to accept his death as a public man (effected by Sophie's dispatch of a premature obituary notice to *The Times*), and seemingly prepare to make the best of a life alone with Caroline.

There is no Dido to add an ambiguous note of optimism to the tragi-comedy of *The Gates of Summer* as she had to the tragedy of *Marching Song*, and the wastes of a shared or separated future dominated by a dead past stretch out before both Hogarth and Caroline—much as Catherine had foreseen them at the climax of *Marching Song*. Only the pathetic Bevis, long Caroline's adorer from afar, offers escape from their shared incarceration, as he, instead of Hogarth, takes her hand at the end of the play. Instead of the clean death accomplished by Rupert Forster—as by Hedvig Ekdal— only the mockery of some Uncle Vanya's poorly aimed pistol shot echoes through the closing gates of John and Caroline's summer.

The comedy is, certainly, a bitter one—its stakes are higher than a penny, and its issues weightier than a song. But it is not quite as bitter as my summary perhaps suggests. Some of the comic elements are in the grotesque vein of *Conditions of Agreement*—even down to the careful semantic incongruity of such a statement as

> Sophie's standing on the terrace kissing a strange old man with a bicycle. [71]

Or in this description by Hogarth of the fury of the London mob in its discovery of his latest amorous intrigue with a publicity-minded bishop's wife:

> They'd got it into their heads that I was breaking up something very dear to their hearts: a home. You know how that country domesticates its idols. The main demonstration was a parade past my house of elderly women carrying banners. That went on for some hours. I felt compelled to send them out tea and sandwiches. They leant against the railings eating and drinking and booing whenever I passed a window. [17]

Eating and drinking and booing—and, one almost expects to hear, clattering their little wooden legs.

The amiably eccentric Selwyn Faramond and Henry Bevis are closer to the comic creations of Whiting in the happier mood of *A Penny for a Song*. Selwyn on the efficacy of church parades for warding off sexual urges ("Made the men rather unhappy turning out so late at night, but it always worked"), [21] or hovering anxiously at the bedroom window, "stark naked, with a pair of field glasses and an improvised megaphone", [26] is close in spirit to Sir Timothy Bellboys. Henry Bevis in his more put-upon moments has his affinities to Lamprett. And Whiting's penchant for such irrelevant but context-giving details as Henry's music hall origins [33–4] and the story Hogarth tantalisingly doesn't quite tell about his sexual initiation, [58] add tongue-in-cheek touches to the humour—and these touches blend with the darker comedy because, I think, they are part of the historic tradition upon which the play draws.

"It is rarely necessary," Whiting might have adapted his earlier remark, "to embroider the finer lunacies of the English at peace." And the English were surely never more assertively, self-consciously at peace than in the years before the outbreak of the First World War. It has become a dramatic fashion, set most firmly and evocatively by John Osborne, to wax nostalgic about this period: but Whiting, while he is indulgent towards its "finer lunacies", recalls that there was a lethargy as well as a sense of certainty about its sun-drenched garden parties—and that the chekhovian malaise of inactivity as well as a deceptive air of leisurely amusement hovered about the tea and honey on the vicarage lawn. I think rightly, he regarded *The Gates of Summer* as "the harshest play I've ever written".[30]

Structurally, *The Gates of Summer* marks a shift away from the unities of time and of place so closely observed in Whiting's earlier plays. There had, admittedly, been a break of three days between the first and second acts of *Conditions of Agreement*, but *Saint's Day* and *A Penny for a Song* completed themselves within twenty-four hours, and *Marching Song* within thirty-six. Here, two days elapse between acts one and two, and, although the second and third take place on the same day, each act has a different location—a complete departure from the single settings which had proved adequate for all Whiting's earlier works.

The set for the first act seems, indeed, to anticipate a similar continuity, for the curtain rises on one of those all-purpose but indefinably "significant" rooms in which all the earlier plays except *A Penny for a Song* had taken place: and there is a characteristically detailed description of the room, almost as if, like the setting for *Saint's Day*, it were shaped from Whiting's experience as well as from his imagination. There is the familiar emphasis on what might be described as *objets trouvés*—"a scarlet shawl thrown over a chair, a piece of jewellery, a gold cross hanging on the egg-shell white wall". But here they are picked out by "the quickening heat" of the sun, not by the half-light filtering through Southman's curtains; and the objects themselves are consonant with the luxury of the decor—a cool, calm luxury, to ease away the stresses of the climate. [5] The first act takes place in the daytime and it is thus important to the mood of the play that it should not be set outside in the sun—otherwise, it could have utilised the same terrace setting as the second act, which takes place when the sun is low and the sombre tone of the action established.

But even the terrace is "enclosed by a low wall". [31] Here, the Emett elements—the archaeological dig, which the designer of *A Penny for a Song* would surely have relished constructing, and the traditional, brawling, sheep-roasting wedding of one of the workmen, which spills over occasionally into the second act [33]—are behind the scenes. And, as if to keep the bright sunlight even more securely shuttered, Whiting sets his last act on the same night as the second, but now in the privacy of John Hogarth's bedroom. With the slightest of shuffling, there would have been no need even for these household scene changes: for Whiting's characters here, like Chekhov's, really require just somewhere to talk. And, after the reminiscing about times past in the first act, the melodramatics in the poisoned present of the second, and the deliberately bathetic anti-climaxes of the third, the tenor of the talking is really what remains of the play. Nobody changes anything. Nobody changes, full stop. There is only a dawning awareness that there will be no change.

Some of Whiting's characters are born exiles, some achieve exile, and some have exile thrust upon them. Sophie and Selwyn Faramond have sought it deliberately; Caroline, the daughter of the roving antiquarian, has been born to it; and Henry Bevis and Hogarth have had it thrust upon them. Such are "the separate ways which brought us here", of which Hogarth speaks to Sophie. "You came in resignation. I've come in affirmation." [11] Even Christos, the one character who is at home in the domestic sense, declares himself spiritually at peace elsewhere—in England, as it happens:

The place fitted my temperament, for I think it must be the saddest country in the world. I long for that perpetual autumn where it is unnecessary—oh, impossible—to face reality: where every leave-taking is performed with the grave courtesy of an obsequy: where the houses look like tombs and the tombs houses: where the mist of bravely unshed tears softens even the harshest gesture. Beautiful! [32]

Whiting, of course, is winking behind those bravely unshed tears. Christos's vignette of autumnal grace is very much how his own and later generations have looked back in nostalgia to England in her Edwardian prime: and in case anybody hasn't measured up the irony for themselves against the tired reality of the English exiles, Christos himself adds that, not being an Englishman, he was "ruined by a desire for excitement", and had to return home after indulging that desire too freely on Epsom Downs. But the seasonal note struck by Christos recurs: there is indeed something of perpetual autumn about the play, and its sadness is underscored rather than muted by the occasional pretence that the gates of summer are truly opening rather than closing. But then the pretence, too, is part of the sadness: it is difficult, as Christos says, to face reality.

In this respect, the title of *The Gates of Summer* is as deceptive as its period. Here is a crucial conversation on the subject between John Hogarth and Caroline—a conversation which is, effectively, a verbal seduction by a young woman of a man who knows that the best is past:

JOHN: All my life I've treated every opportunity as the last chance. I've looked—oh, sadly—on each encounter as the last. But I was cheated. The sun came up and the sun went down and, damn it, life had to be lived. And opportunity didn't knock once. It beat a positive tattoo at my door.

CAROLINE: Which every time you opened.

JOHN: It was never shut. (*He kisses her on the forehead.*) But now the foot of time is edging it to. Soon there'll only be space in the doorway for the lightest and most frivolous opportunity to get through. The last—the smallest and least consequential—will have to stay, I suppose, to

comfort my extreme age for there'll be no getting out.
CAROLINE: My God! Can't you——(*John kisses her on the mouth.*)—see? Can't you see—that before you—haven't you eyes?—oh yes! you've eyes—before you is not a quickly closing door. No, John—darling, my new found one: der—fool! there before you are the wide open gates of summer. You've lived only—nothing but—the early months of your year of life. Stay on. I'll not mind—never mind—if you go on from me to another—fairer, she may be—but be aware—be'ware—not old, not sleeping but now whilst young—of the fairest to hand. Stay. Go on from me—after all—if you want to go —on. Go on. [29]

But Caroline—she of the slurred, elliptical baby-talk, and the little pun-like meaning-twists which try so hard to sound endearing—is deceiving herself, as she is trying to deceive John.

Catherine had hoped that Dido would teach her how to live again: just so, Caroline, remembering the "wild unorthodox stories" of Greece told her in her convent school, hoped that "this might be the place to bring me alive again". She even believes that "it's done so". And Hogarth replies:

I know what you mean. You become aware. Yes? Am I right? Aware that you're taking up space and that the sun exists to strike down and enwrap you. Aware that you are here! Alive, wound up—more—working, ticking, going. Registering something more than a mood. Yes. It's a discovery to be reckoned with, I agree. Life is not, after all, founded on the meal table, the privy and the bed. [27]

Hogarth himself has come to Greece in search of the same resurrection of self, the same heightening of awareness. But the test of his own and of Caroline's optimism is in the living of these vaunted new lives. "Age doesn't come into it," as Caroline has already said. "You can be finished at twenty-four." And she is twenty-five—knowing, as Hogarth expresses his own sense of the past, the "feeling of sadness for what I loved" which is the feeling of the spiritually exhausted. [12–13] Nothing in the play transcends this sadness—in other words, nothing in the new lives of Caroline and John diminishes their overwhelming sense of what is beyond recall, but not beyond regret.

There could scarcely be a more appropriate setting for a play in which people are forever burrowing into their pasts than one about (or rather one whose geographical location is excused by) archaeology. But if Selwyn Faramond is seeking the raw material of history for museums, Christos is rewriting Sophie's personal past as it might have been, and Sophie fails to notice the difference—except, perhaps, in the evenings:

CHRISTOS: Her memory at this time of day is too accurate for comfort.

JOHN: Surely that's what you want.

CHRISTOS: Accuracy about the past! Mr Hogarth, you speak like a scholar.

JOHN: Is there another value in reminiscence?

CHRISTOS: Certainly. A record of what might have been.

JOHN: In that case, where does the truth get to?

CHRISTOS: Now you speak, sir, as if the truth was a considerable detail. The book will only be read by the future.

JOHN: Then Sophie's life in London is a myth.

CHRISTOS: It will be by the time I've got it on paper. [44]

"The future," as Sophie herself puts it of her husband, with heavy, resigned irony, "definitely seems to lie in the past." [73]

Sophie is no longer much interested in John Hogarth—except as a character in her book, and, as such, the nature of his death is a matter for the authoress's discretion rather than the real John's choice or chance. She does at one point consider that death by poisoning might make "a much better ending" for him than death on the battlefield: [55] but in the end she decides that "falling gallantly at the head of your native troops led gallantly in a lost cause" will suffice, and she sends her telegram to *The Times* accordingly. [74] For the first time Hogarth finds that he is enmeshed in Sophie's mythic version of himself, and, there being no preferable alternative, he accepts the loss of freely-willed identity.

Hogarth, although he imagines briefly that he is going to make war as well as love, chooses his war carefully. "The affair is small enough," he remarks, "for me to play a big part". [10] His own acceptance of responsibility is thus strictly limited by his capacity for deriving amused kudos from it. So it is perhaps significant that he describes "the language of action", with which Basilios had at last stirred his dormant soul, as "a language I've known since childhood. Yet until that night I'd never heard it spoken". [10] And there is more than a hint of longing for childish things in Hogarth's chosen route for travelling back into the past. Trying to shake off Caroline's attentions, he tells her: "My appointment is not with you, I'm afraid. It's with a man who took me by the hand and dragged me from childhood—all those broken toys, remember—to this present time. Basilios." [19] But the rejection of childish things which he is here attempting cannot be sustained in the night-light of Basilios's grand charade.

In the terms of Hogarth's metaphor, the "broken toys" are, of course, the cast-off mistresses of whom he has grown tired:

> JOHN: All the best games end in destruction.
> CAROLINE: We never get out of the nursery where everything finishes broken up. You played the whole of your life in London that way, didn't you? Without seriousness, because you knew the time would come when you'd have to put your toys away. So better smash them! You were right. You were quite right. [17–18]

But Hogarth wasn't right at all. As it turns out, he has merely given up a destructive sexual game for one more elaborate, which proves more difficult to bring to an abrupt end. Caroline is nearer to the truth about both of them when she says that they "never get out of the nursery". And the recurrent imagery of perpetuated childhood bears this out. From Hogarth's farewell present to Sophie of a musical box ("something to be given to a child—or to me"), [12] to the pistol with which he practises his poor marksmanship ("You'll not save your life with that kind of toy," says Caroline), [31] the trappings of Hogarth's life are reduced to those of a boyhood game.

This inevitably recalls the dominant mood of play-acting and practical joking in *Conditions of Agreement*, and the petulance which was its only motive force. And Caroline, sure enough, is as adept at vicious trickery as Nicholas—although she has had more experience of purring when this achieves her ends than her crippled forebear. Now, she is playing a doubly-ironic game with Hogarth—the game of poisoning, which turns out to be a make-believe, though she had imagined it, at last, to be real. Similarly, she has played just such a cruelly calculated trick on the dumbly adoring Bevis, when, unable to speak the language of the natives, he has asked Caroline to translate his questions about "local habits and customs" to a group they meet out riding. Bevis is promptly set upon and beaten up: but when captured the supposed assassins

> swore that Caroline had told them I was a wealthy Turk travelling the country buying up young girls—in this case their daughters—for immoral purposes. [49]

Nicholas would have relished that. It is, says Caroline, "what the Henrys are for"—to be "made unhappy". [36]

Poor Henry: he has a theory that every man has his own capacity for responsibility. "I don't think I'm big enough to take on a revolution as Hogarth's doing," he tells Caroline, "but I think I could help you." [15] Little does he realise—and little does Hogarth realise, come to that—how impossible are both demands. As it turns out, it's uncertain whether it is Hogarth who is left to manage Caroline, and Bevis who is sent off to report the revolution, or vice-versa. "Did you really think the game with Caroline could be ended by knocking over the board?" asks Sophie. [53] Hogarth had indeed hoped so—and so, with her poisoned wine, had Caroline. But neither has had any influence whatsoever on the situation which leaves them confronting a disillusioned future as the last-act curtain falls.

And the falling of the curtain is the closing of the gates of summer. That eponymous image recurs as Basilios reflects on the absurd happiness his garden-party in honour of his last mistress has brought him. "With her hands she closed the gates of love behind me," he tells Hogarth, [68] of that unseen courtesan whose grandiose schemes are turned sour in the savouring, just like Caroline's. There is something predatory about all the women in the play, as there had been about all the men in *Conditions of Agreement*: but at least here the victims are willing, and come to that have little else to do but submit. They have little else to do: period.

In almost the longest speech in the play, Hogarth thus describes the kind of "reasonable" day he has been wont to spend, year in and year out, "day by day by night time" in London. The only creative activity it has contained has been that of the playhouse: and "the curtain rattles down on the play and the day. Hohum!" [18] This speech of Hogarth's takes his typical twenty-four hours full-circle, back to its carbon-copy commencement—just as the play itself takes him full-circle back to the routine of sex from which he has been trying to escape:

> CAROLINE: I'd say there's nothing left for you but to be happy. Sad, isn't it?
>
> JOHN: And what is there left for you?
>
> CAROLINE: You. Or have you some other commitment of honour to fulfil?
>
> JOHN: No. I've nothing at all. Not even money now. What do you say to that? People always thought I was a rich man. I was not. I had an indulgent mother.
>
> CAROLINE: Could you work?
>
> JOHN: That's unkind.
>
> CAROLINE: I didn't mean it.
>
> JOHN: Yes you did. You were looking at me as if I'm a pack horse you're about to load. You're not going to send me out to work Caroline. That's one thing nobody's ever suggested. [70]

In Chekhov's plays, too, everybody is always talking about work and never doing any: and here, the single reference to work is in this passage, where it is dismissed as the "one thing nobody's ever suggested". Selwyn's archaeology is merely a dilettante hobby: the only person in the play who does work *for a living* is Henry Bevis. And he's a figure of fun, to be "made unhappy".

This resolute turning of backs upon the possibilities of work is one of the elements which makes *The Gates of Summer* a comedy, for all its evident astringency. Tragedy can afford to leave no option open: here, all the options are open, but there's still only one thing to be done. And so, if the second-act curtain has a foretaste of *Waiting for Godot* about it:

> JOHN: May I just speak?
> The two women attend to him. There is a long silence. [55]

Then the third-act curtain—Caroline's fingers snapping "imperiously" as her bare arm emerges from the bed curtains, in anticipation of a lifetime of "getting on with it"— is more reminiscent of *Huis Clos*:

> CAROLINE: May I ask one question? Just one.
> JOHN: Yes.
> CAROLINE: I want to know. Do we all get what we deserve?
> JOHN: Yes. (*He is at the door.*)
> CAROLINE: Every time?
> JOHN: Yes. [75]

There the action ends. Caroline has spoken her own epitaph:

> However splendid the pursuit, and however corrupt the trickery, I'll end up with a man. Just a man. [75]

Now the illusion and the trickery are over. Caroline *has* ended up with "just a man". Similarly, Selwyn's hoped-for monument to an inspired faith has turned out to be a temple of "inspired graffiti", which only show that little has changed in the exercise of one of man's animal functions. Indeed, it is precisely the permanency of the sexual illusion which is celebrated in John Hogarth's mock-article for Henry Bevis's readers describing the discoveries—incidentally the longest speech in the play. [57-9] And John's hoped-for revolution has turned out to be the last pathetic fumblings for power of a clique of reactionary, squabbling old men.

Both *Marching Song* and *The Gates of Summer* are set, as it were, above the battle—*Marching Song* in the historical aftermath of an actual and momentous conflict, *The Gates of Summer* in the unrealised anticipation of a struggle which, had it even taken place, would have been brief and abortive. It's as if, in qualifying every affirmation in *Marching Song* with its moral question-mark, Whiting had felt that his earlier play nevertheless remained too sure of itself in the single assumption that was never doubted—the assumption that it all, somehow, mattered. For in *The Gates of Summer* nothing matters very much. Conversely, it is also as if Whiting had felt that *A Penny for a Song* was too rosily inconsequential: and so here he shows that inconsequence can itself be cruel as well as comic.

Of course it's doubtful whether Whiting ever thought, consciously at least, anything so schematic: and to label his first comedy a *pièce rose* and his second and last a *pièce noire* would thus be to tell, say, only two-thirds of the truth. Yet that there is something over-structured about them is undeniable and unfortunate. If the resolution of *Marching Song* is arguably too simple, then the anti-climax of *The Gates of Summer* is certainly too complicated—or perhaps this is just a way of saying that the play in which nothing happens proved harder to write than the one in which a great deal does. At least, as one watches the gates of summer closing and senses the nip of autumnal frost in the air, one can't help remembering the harvest festival of *A Penny for a Song* more kindly than the withered crops of *The Gates of Summer*.

4

Children of Misfortune

No Why, A Walk in the Desert and *The Devils*

No Why and *A Walk in the Desert* are both one-acters—short breaks in the self-imposed silence between Whiting's early writing for the theatre and the commission from Peter Hall to write what proved to be his last completed play, *The Devils*. *No Why* was first in order of composition—it was written in 1957, and intended as a curtain-raiser to Whiting's own translation of Anouilh's *Traveller Without Luggage*. But it was the last to be staged, in a posthumous production in the first *Expeditions* programme at the Aldwych in 1964.

The least substantial of Whiting's published plays, *No Why* is not only extremely short—the script fills barely a dozen pages—but spare in style, and thin in its sense of theatre. It is nevertheless useful to remind oneself that the play was written before the absurdist wave had really broken upon the English theatre—and it anticipates, in particular, that device of using an unspeaking central character who acts as a catalyst for the revelation of all kinds of guilt, which was used with more assurance if not much greater success in Pinter's *A Slight Ache*.

The silent hero of *No Why* is Jacob, a child of unspecified age who has committed an unspecified crime. It is, one deduces, evidently of the trivial, perhaps obliquely sexual sort that older-style parents are apt to think of as "nasty": in any case, its perpetrator must have his face rubbed in his supposed guilt, because he has dredged up all kinds of submerged memories of the infancy of his elders. The panacea is, of course, "saying you're sorry", which Jacob refuses to do, his numbed passivity unnerving the grown-ups —cousin, aunts, and a senile grandfather joining the parental inquisition in the attic during the course of the action—until their alternate wheedling and nagging verges on hysteria.

Towards the end of the play the father is left alone with the child, and, in a last burst of recrimination, finds that a second voice—his own, yet amplified and independent— is joining in the abuse. *His* father's voice, perhaps? One can extrapolate whatever detail is most helpful in comprehending how guilt can thus be put on a pedestal, almost an effect apart from its cause—elaborated out of all importance, and, in the process, ironically transferred to its would-be expiators. The final image is of the child alone, the outline of his body dimly emerging from the darkness in which his father has, of course, left him, swinging from the cord of his pyjamas. Jacob has hanged himself.

Whiting betrays considerable uncertainty in handling this plot material. He seems unable to decide on whom the action is to be focused—whether on the badgering parents, who often appear to have created the child from their own obsessed imaginations, or on Jacob himself. For if the child truly does have an objective existence, what is the theatrical point of his stylisation as an inert dummy? And what is the significance of his eventual progress downstage, into the light, just before he commits suicide? Whiting's stage direction is as follows:

Jacob gets up from the chair. He comes forward and stares

D

into the theatre. He waits, as if for a word. Do any of us speak? No. And if we did, what would we say? [92]

This is one of Whiting's least inspired foreshadowings of theatrical conventions, reminiscent of all the later guilt-ridden plays—prominent among them Peter Brook's *US*, that quasi-documentary interpretation of the Vietnam War as a symptom of liberal masochism—in which actors have taken it upon their transcendent selves to accuse their audiences, but have usually succeeded only in making them conscious of the imminent interval instead of increasing their awareness of "real" issues at stake.

This quibble, in relation to *No Why*, is a minor one, but it's suggestive of Whiting's uncertainty of direction. "Do any of us speak?" Of course not: it would be most disconcerting for the juvenile actor playing the part of Jacob were we to raise a liberal outcry. "And if we did, what would we say?" Well, perhaps something like: look here, sonny, first of all tell us if you're just a figment of your parents' imagination—for if you are, you've no business to be here now they've gone. If you're not, was your silence a symbol or a symptom? And was their anger how it seemed to you, how it really was, or how it seemed to them?

Wherever the truth lies—the theatrical truth, that is—it's surely not far from the commonplace. At least, where the play *is* explicit, it's neither illuminating nor very original. "Come on, you want to grow up, don't you?" asks the sycophantic cousin. "Then say: I'm sorry." [84] To grow up, one interprets, is to be sorry—for one's existence? Evidently. "What's he done?" asks Grandfather, as well he might. "He exists, Father," replies Aunt Amy, shortly. "Look at him, there in front of your face. He is, Father." [90]

More precisely, perhaps, Aunt Amy means that Jacob now dares to exist *independently* of his parents—or so it is suggested in his father's tiresomely coarse fantasy about the child's babyhood, before he became "this little criminal".

Remember how happy we were? Remember the long winter evenings as we sat reading the school year-book and careers for boys and he lay farting in his cot? [86]

It's no good. That typical device of lulling an audience with a string of connectives and then startling it with an unexpected phrase strikes one as too easy a trick this time round: and it's not even in character. In any case, the Mother is right to disabuse her husband. "It was all from the very start for our sake, not for his," she says. [86] Thus, when the Father returns in the morning he says he hopes "to find my real little boy. The boy I want to love." [92] That, of course, is presumably how he will be found—dead clay, for the moulding of parental fantasies. Yet, Jacob has, effectively, been nothing more than dead clay throughout the action—there is no contrast, no expressive counterpoint between the "criminal" assertion of his individuality and his actual inertia; or between his life, as it's represented on stage, and his death. Maybe this is the point—but if so, it's one of far too many possible points, which systematically cancel each other out, just as they cancel out our own responses to the play.

No Why retains a certain interest as a study in verbal rape, and some of its embellishments—the cloying, incestuous mother-love of Jacob's cousin, for instance—strike off at allusive tangents. But whereas the injection of such apparently superfluous details enriches others of Whiting's plays, here they are accretions which scar the already flimsy surface tissue of the action. Ronald Hayman discusses the play as a prolegomena to *The Devils*—in which, also, evil masquerades as good, and its perpetrators are determined to extract a "confession" for their satisfaction.[31] This idea is persuasive within the wider context of Whiting's work: but in explaining *No Why* as a play in its own right, I can't help feeling it also explains it away.

A Walk in the Desert was written for television in 1959 and screened in the following year: intended to fill a sixty-minute slot, it adapts with minimal alterations into a fairly substantial one-acter for the stage. Only the outdoor filmed sequences, which place the action in its social context of the upper-middle class neighbourhood of a "small town in the Midlands", need to be cut, and a multiple set can readily be constructed to accommodate the drawing-room, dining-room and hallway of the Sharpe household. (The interior decoration is described by Whiting as "haute bourgeoisie: 1930", making this the only play of his which has the conventional trappings of drawing-room drama.) [97] Whiting himself thought of *A Walk in the Desert* as a revamping of *Conditions of Agreement*: but the two plays have little in common—in so far as this can be said of any of Whiting's works—except that a practical joke played by a cripple is the mainspring of both their actions.

Peter Sharpe, though twenty-four, still dawdles away his time in his parents' home. Having lost a leg while doing his National Service—not in military action, but in a senseless accident involving an army lorry—he occupies himself trying to goad his mother and father into some sort of response other than well-bred inanity, and deriving a small satisfaction from what is evidently his only friendship, with a man more than ten years older than himself called Tony Coleman. As the action begins, Peter's parents are just off for an evening of amateur dramatics, and Tony is about to pay one of his regular visits.

The pair talk desultorily and scene-settingly until the unexpected arrival of a strange girl, Shirley Flanders, whom Peter greets at the front door. Shirley has, in fact, come to the wrong house, in answer to an advertisement for a secretary by the successful author—a boyhood friend of Peter's—who lives next door. Peter talks to the girl alone in another room, until he judges it impossible for Tony to thwart his intention of posing as the prospective employer: then, in the course of the "interview", he browbeats Shirley's most shaming secret out of her—she is the mother of an illegitimate baby—before packing her off, too late to get the genuine job. It has just been "something to do". [110]

Peter and Tony quarrel over the deception, raking to the surface the real, shallow nature of their mutual dependence. Peter's parents return, ambulances and fire-engines race by: a body, the Sharpes think, has been found in the canal. Tony and Peter think of the disappointed, humiliated Shirley: but neither goes out to investigate. "You're trying to stop it being true by not finding out," accuses Peter. [128]

Anybody who didn't know the play, or didn't know Whiting, would probably by now have assumed two things: that the "real nature" of Peter and Tony's friendship was homosexual, and that the ghost of Shirley was, indeed, fated to overshadow both their futures. But even allowing for the date of the play—when any homosexual relationship on television would perforce have been portrayed evasively, or transposed into ostensibly heterosexual terms—there is no hint that either of the two men is sexually, as distinct from socially, abnormal. And—more important than mere avoidance of that obvious cliché—Shirley turns up, alive and alert, to collect the handbag she'd forgotten in the stress of departure. Now quite collected again, she asks:

> Why can't you people take things as they are? Look at you now. Inventing a sad story for me. She ended up in the river. It'd never be like that. Never. [130]

Shirley is right. The play is an elaborate game of consequences: but the consequences are merely those of practical jokes—or of other such arbitrary, purposeless accidents as Peter's—and no more significant. Indeed, in this case, even the effects are trivial or transient.

A Walk in the Desert gets its title from a reference in one of Peter's last speeches to the "joke"—a joke he's not enjoying— of his present existence:

> I mean living in a desert like this. At one time I believed that this waste ground must have boundaries. And I thought that if I made my way towards that limit I'd at last meet with people. Well, there's been Tony. And there was Roy and Harry—remember Harry?—and others. But as soon as I took their hand and prepared myself to love them, what did I find? They were not at the beginning of a fertile land, but making for some other, more believable, place than I had in mind. So the most we could do was pass each other, without doing more harm than was necessary. [132]

There is a beckettian ring to Peter's crippled crawl across the waste—although the desert, in this case, is identifiably his home town. But the Peters of the world make each their own wilderness. That is why Shirley becomes first a plaything, then "an enemy". She "believes in the good land. I don't any more. Not the chance of reaching it, anyway. So I tried to stop her. We fought on shifting ground with no result." [133] No result. As in *Conditions of Agreement* and *The Gates of Summer*, so here—no result.

But there has been a shifting of ground on the playwright's part. There is a more sustained attempt at psychological rationalisation, and at putting things into a semi-naturalistic context—in part, possibly, a result of adjustment to the medium of television, but in view of Whiting's increasing concern in *The Devils* with the physical side of pain, more probably a deliberate change in thematic emphasis. In all the earlier plays the action mattered more than its actor. This meant that there was relatively less interest in pain and death as a climax to human individuality than in its dramatic function as the logical culmination to a sequence of events. Thus, the interest in *Marching Song* was in the *rationale* of Rupert's dying, not in the nature or the act of his death, which is almost incidental: and in *The Gates of Summer*, both Caroline and Hogarth, imagining themselves poisoned, were entirely unconcerned with what promised to be the lengthy *process* of dying—for they were too much taken up with the causes and consequences of the accomplished act.

In *A Walk in the Desert*, however, pain *as such* has become an important aspect of the human response. And this personalises the issues more vividly than is usual in Whiting's work: in *Conditions of Agreement*, for example, it was not so much what made Nicholas and Peter wrongdoers or A.G. their wronged victim that mattered, but rather their *acts* of wrongdoing. Here, Peter describes himself in his relationship with Shirley in precisely these terms: they are "the wrongdoer and the wronged". [118] But in so doing he becomes Whiting's most fully self-aware practical-joker. Merely to be self-aware is not, of course, in itself to turn towards or be deflected from a path of self-destruction. Existence precedes essence: but is that existence shaped by accident or by choice?

The one character who doesn't really fit into the play's moral framework is Tony Coleman. True, he is necessary, as accomplice and confidant: and as a type—the prematurely middle-ageing bachelor, seeking to recapture his youth vicariously, but permitted only the company of such misfits as Peter—he is believable enough. But when his condition is particularised, and he explains his loneliness, he achieves pathos without personality, [104–5] and he is too important a character for this not to matter. "Why didn't you tell me it was a joke?" Shirley asks him, and Peter echoes the question: but it is never answered, either by Tony or from what we know of him. [119–20]

Shirley herself, on the other hand, is surprisingly acceptable—surprisingly, because she is probably the most uncomplicatedly ordinary character ever created by a dramatist who, as a self-confessed elitist, was out of sympathy with ordinary people (and who preferred, in any case, extraordinary themes). Yet Shirley strikes a nice balance between her representative role and her individuality. Her defence of her family and of its values carries conviction without being over-articulate. [113] And her desire for ordinariness becomes the more coherent because she is now denied it: for she is devoted to the care of her child and of her father from a sense of guilt as much as from love. But she is still ordinary enough not to lose hope. "I'll find somebody", she believes: and even after Peter's tirade forces her to concede her loneliness and its likely persistence, she asserts, "suddenly very tired",

Well, I don't know. All I do know is that you've got to go
on somehow. [118–19]

This is all that Peter means by Shirley's belief in "the good
land". And this is why her return is dramatically as well
as functionally necessary. Already, Shirley has bounced
back. Peter has failed to make her share his own sense of
total isolation: "some sort of joke" has been played, [119]
but it has had "no result".

As in *The Gates of Summer*, the purpose of the joke is not
merely that of seeking a fellow-sufferer by means of creating
one. What happened, as Tony says in the final quarrel with
Peter, would have happened anyway:

If you were active and got around, if Mummie and
Daddie understood you, if you were a success like Brian,
it wouldn't make any difference. You'd still want to
have somebody concerned in some way with you. Perhaps
not in your misery, but in something equally trivial, such
as your happiness. Yes, with you up and about and she a
bit prettier . . . you'd probably have made love to her
instead of doing what you did. But either way it's a
crime. Engaging another person's emotions to prove that
you exist. [123]

If Shirley had been a bit prettier, and a little more self-
possessed, she might almost have been Patience in *Conditions
of Agreement*. And here, indeed, is circumstantial evidence
of a conscious remoulding of that source material, for Whiting
has thus fused the roles of Patience as observer and A.G. as
victim, so that Shirley becomes both a personal and a
sexual stranger to Peter. But I'm not sure that the loss of
complexity in the tensions of the personal relationships

is quite compensated for by the greater probability of Peter's imposition, and of his motives for it.

"I wanted her to feel something about me. . . . Something positive," Peter confesses: but in Tony's repudiation of his action he loses even the illusion of a "positive" friendship. [122] Tony "gave up long ago" engaging the emotions of others. He's "quite happy to drift on the surface of other people's lives". [123] As for Peter's father, even the emotion of hatred or an act of unkindness are now hard to elicit from him. "If he could have been so definite," Peter reflects, "I think I could have loved him."

> But I was nothing to him. The creature he passed on the stairs, the thing underneath his feet which longed to be kicked, but he had no time even for cruelty. [127]

His father had no time . . . and Peter has all the time in the world, to devote to trying himself out on other people's feelings. "I thought you'd think it was funny," he complains to Tony. "Something to do. Pass the time. You're always talking about it." [121]

Tony has, indeed, been talking about it. "You mustn't think of Peter in terms of people visiting him, or being sorry for him," he has told Mr Sharpe. "He just wants what we all want. A bit of company, a laugh, some way of passing the time." [100–1] And Peter himself remarks that his father's play-acting "passes the time", [98] a godotesque echo that rings through the whole play. Thus, for Peter, playing a practical joke is better than doing nothing, and it may even stimulate a passing acquaintance. Whether to hatred or to love doesn't matter all that much:

> But it has been some sort of encounter. It's made a landmark, something to catch the eye, like litter on the hills.

Something to occupy my mind as I go—forward?—in this labyrinth without walls. Something to remember. Something. . . . [133]

And on this image, of a beckettian landscape of brief encounters during directionless wanderings, the curtain falls.

There is one sense in which *A Walk in the Desert* continues the study of parental possessiveness rather unsatisfactorily begun in *No Why*. For Peter claims that his supposed friendship with Tony was "an invention" of his parents. "Like most things I possess." [129] And the later play does show up the insufficiency of the earlier in this respect. "Inventing" a relationship is no parental prerogative—and Peter himself "invents" a tragic death for Shirley. "Why can't you people take things as they are?" Shirley has asked: [130] and the question is meant for Peter and all his kind, flung back at the man who had said of Shirley's lower middle class road full of lower middle class houses: "They're inhabited by peasants. Why don't they have the honesty of peasants?" [112]

What Shirley has achieved is not so much honesty as the certain comfort of her fatalism. And because her fatalism has little to do with morality, it need not be self-destructive. Consider this exchange, which is opened by Peter with a characteristic question about the "moral" consequences of Shirley's unmarried motherhood:

PETER: Are you going to atone for it?
SHIRLEY: I don't think I quite know what that means. I'm going to make up for it.
PETER: Not the same thing.
SHIRLEY: What I mean is . . . well, look at you. Somewhere

you collected that leg of yours. But you haven't let it
hold you back. You've gone on and made a success with
your book. Good for you, I say.
PETER: This—(*his leg*)—wasn't my fault.
SHIRLEY: Your fault? What are you talking about?
Things happen. They just happen. I've learnt that
by now. Haven't you? [115]

Peter hasn't learnt it—he hasn't, of course, written a book,
or done anything else much. Agonising existentially about
how he "happened to be in a certain place at a certain
time" [115] has sapped the "peasant honesty" which is
Shirley's optimism in the face of "things happening"—
as, earlier, it might have been Dido's.

    This points to a central paradox in Whiting's work. He
was a self-proclaimed member of an elite, writing for an
elite: and yet so much in his plays amounts to a cautionary
tale against the dangers of spiritual atrophy that are atten-
dant upon losing the common touch. An elite may be right—
as Southman was right. It may be noble, as Forster was
noble, or prepared to sacrifice life and fortune, as was John
Hogarth. Yet it lives at one remove from "peasant honesty"
and so deceives itself—or, more dangerously, at one remove
from life, and so destroys itself. In Whiting's plays the simple
people—the child Stella, the grown-up children of *Penny for
a Song*, the instinctive Dido, even the buffoon Bevis in a play
that is otherwise unrelievedly pessimistic, and now the
peasant Shirley—are those whose lives at least hint at a
childlike hope. The others retain of childhood its tantrums,
and forget its trust.

    In *The Devils*—commissioned and written in 1960, and
produced as the first new play to be staged by the Royal
Shakespeare Company at the Aldwych early in the following

year—the tantrums of another of Whiting's "children of misfortune" work themselves out in another practical joke. And because the action is set in the past rather than the present, and in the field of public affairs rather than of private feuds, the consequences of the joke are fatal albeit, arguably, no less inconsequential. Greeted as little short of a masterpiece, *The Devils* strikes one, in retrospect, as a tired, almost dispirited piece of writing, manipulating stage effects and emotional dead-certainties to achieve a deceptive forcefulness on stage. In most of Whiting's work the core is so dense that gravity plays funny tricks at the crust: but here the inner world of the play is too flimsy to support the intensity of action on its surface. And the result is melodrama.

Whiting had written of *A Penny for a Song* that "all it states, in very simple terms, is the idea of Christian charity".[32] *The Devils*, apparently, has to do with Christian hypocrisy. Its story of suspected diabolism at Loudun in seventeenth-century France had already been told in the Polish film *Mother Joan of the Angels*, and in Aldous Huxley's documentary-style narrative *The Devils of Loudun*. Whiting based this, his first and only historical play, on the latter source[33]— offering, in alternative fulfilment of Peter Hall's commission, to attempt a version of Frederick Rolfe's *Hadrian VII*.[34] He wanted, in short, to write either about the turbulent priest Grandier of history, or about a would-be turbulent priest of fantasy-autobiography. And, in passssing, it's worth noting that Peter Luke's later adaptation of *Hadrian* enjoyed very much the same kind of popular success as did *The Devils*—since both plays, along with, for example, Robert Bolt's *A Man for All Seasons* and John Osborne's *Luther*, follow a particular fashion in dramatising history. Whether one would be justified in suggesting that Whiting at this stage of his life needed the impetus of existing raw material to sustain his own writing it's now impossible to tell. But if his earlier plays are those of a pioneer striking ahead of his fellows to explore new frontiers, *The Devils* is more like the work of a man conscientiously following in the footsteps of others.

A programme note to the original Aldwych production summarised the historical facts:

> In 1617 a priest called Urbain Grandier was appointed to the important living of Saint-Pierre-du-Marché at Loudun, a town of central France. He was then twenty-seven, brilliant, handsome, ambitious—and lecherous. . . . Not surprisingly, his downfall, when it came, came by way of a woman; more surprisingly, it was a woman whom Grandier had not even seen, let alone seduced. This was Soeur Jeanne des Anges, prioress of a convent of seventeen Ursuline nuns, a young woman with little true religious vocation. She had heard of Grandier's amorous exploits, and her imagination was dangerously excited by them. The priest became her secret obsession, and the obsession spread, with results that were grotesque, grim and for Grandier fatal.

As Whiting himself commented,

> The situation is simply that local superstition—politics, fear, revenge—all subscribe to the fact that people come to believe it, and he is arrested, tried and burned. Now, that's all it is. Well, I mean this could all be put down on half a page. But the thing is a play, somebody's got to say something and therefore one has got to find the significant points in it and a shape. Where do you start? Well, I have started in the gutter. I mean literally in the gutter, and the play gets up out of it.[35]

I'm not sure that it ever really does. As Huxley had noted, "sex mingles easily with religion, and their blending has one of those slightly repulsive and yet exquisite and poignant flavours which startle the palate like a revelation—of what?" Whiting, however, found little that was poignant or exquisite in his material: and what there is can be separated-out too readily from what he found—or made—repulsive.

Though still formally in three acts—of all Whiting's plays, the short pieces apart, only *A Penny for a Song* had been squeezed into two—the action of *The Devils* moves episodically within a loose scenic framework of the streets of Loudun, the homes of its citizens, and its civic and religious institutions. Grandier's early, casual sleeping-around settles into an apparently more enduring relationship with the public prosecutor's daughter, Phillipe, but this is cut short cruelly, in all senses, by her pregnancy—and finally by Grandier's torture and death, after the lengthy, rival investigations of church and state into his alleged diabolism.

The plottings of the priest's enemies and the grindings of bureaucratic machinery contrast with the cavortings of the possessed nuns—who claim Grandier as their diabolic guide—to form a background that is richly detailed yet somehow opaque. The essential scene-setting is done with unobtrusive economy: but the play is thematically as dense as *Saint's Day*, its action drawing in all sorts of peripheral people and events. (The cast list cites by name nearly two dozen characters.) At one of its better-buried levels it is even "about" that paper tiger of an issue, clerical celibacy, which is perfunctorily documented and psychologised, Grandier himself having written in favour of the marriage of priests [196]—although his special pleading in the matter doesn't quite fit the prophet of protestantism, warning of "the men who will come after me", who must be convinced not by torture but by argument. [216] *The Devils* is also about religious bigotry—yet the *reductio ad absurdum* of intolerance in the scenes of inquisition and exorcism, which casually juxtapose the tragic and the farcical in the manner of a medieval mystery play, tends to jar on a contemporary sensibility. One *knows* how wicked and gruesome it all was: one *feels* the need to understand, to have things not merely condemned but considered, not excused but examined.

Thus, a chemist and a surgeon, Adam and Mannoury, are the chief petty plotters against Grandier: and the caricaturist's glee with which they are drawn suggests Whiting's intention of fixing the past by using its own conventions— as also his elitist's spite against a bourgeoisie rampant and, in the end, triumphant. But if the bourgeoisie are buffoons, condemning their priest's sexuality whilst revelling in aristocratic debaucheries from which they get a professional rake-off, [147] Father Barré, exorcist extraordinary— with his slanging matches with evil spirits, and his prophecies of "happiness in hell tonight" [183] when he is temporarily thwarted—is never more than a pasteboard priest, just as Grandier's chief clerical opponent, De la Rochepozay, is a pasteboard prelate. The trouble is that, although the pasteboard has the bold resilience of a tolerably comic postcard, it is out of a different sort of play from Grandier himself—and, not insignificantly, dialectical confrontations between the chief character and these caricatures are virtually avoided.

The plot is further complicated by the side-issue of state interference, instigated by Richelieu, in the city privileges of Loudun, and by the setting up of a rival court of enquiry into the diabolism, which threatens to interfere with Father Barré's eagerness to find the devil in everybody's works. But the suspense this latter device creates is all too close to that of the courtroom whodunit. And one's suspicions of sub-plotting for distraction's sake are heightened by the fact that the first rival court (which declares that the nuns are merely hysterical and Grandier innocent) does its work offstage, whilst the second, more spectacular intervention of De Condé [193–4] is relished in detail. For De Condé's unconventional methods of revealing the nun's deceptions are highly theatrical: but they advance the religious dialectic not one step. Their effect is simply to shift one's attention from Grandier as a strongly individualised tragic figure, in acute religious perplexity, to his misfortunes as a victim of circumstance.

In filling out his play to an ostensibly epic scale, Whiting has thus failed to fit his hero into the tragi-comic social framework—indeed, one's natural tendency to think of Grandier in "heroic" terms suggests that he is not a suitable figure for epic treatment at all. And the bits and pieces of social criticism and of commonplace caricature, though intermittently successful as fragments from some living newspaper of the renaissance, are trying too hard to be more than the sum of their parts to be truly epic either.

So there are really two plays here—sometimes separately identifiable, as if the scenes had just got jumbled together, but more often as if the realistic hero from one play has got involved with other kinds of characters altogether. The bulk of the cast is taking part in an epic piece about political and clerical corruption—about the failures of man as a social animal, the self-deceptions and conscious hypocrisies of the better or worse members of a supposedly God-fearing community. This first play does not even attempt to point to universal truths: its characters are too close to their society ever to transcend its particular values, and are in any case more puppets than people. "What a lot of criticism we middle classes come in for just because we like things nice," says Adam the chemist, [160] and the quality of the irony is as representative as its irrelevance to Grandier's spiritual predicament. Thus, the caricatures are not redeemed by much wittiness or originality of treatment, nor even by any sharply critical insight on their creator's part. For the social and political evils they personify are of no more than historical interest, although their shaping is all too evidently —and here lies the crucial contradiction—the product of a twentieth-century mind: the attitude to history is thus whig and tory all at once, and the distinctive insights offered separately by these approaches are alike lost. The first of the parallel plays is neither interestingly historical nor pertinently didactic. The socio-religious forces ranged against Grandier thus become much less powerful-seeming as enemies: and whilst it is psychologically appropriate that Grandier's real enemy should be himself, this does call into question the substance of one half of the play, and the epic structure of the whole of it.

Occasionally there are hints of an overlap between the two planes of action—on one occasion a physical overlap, which takes place on the city fortifications between (downstage) Grandier and his patron D'Armagnac, and (in the distance) Louis XIII and Richelieu. This enables D'Armagnac, remarking of Richelieu that "when a man's intent on power . . . he can justify his actions with absurdities", [156] to suggest the kind of slanting of the action that could have interrelated its religio-bureaucratic, civic, and personal themes. But even in this scene, affairs of state are merely subjects for caricature—Louis's clay-like malleability in Richelieu's hands actually being illustrated by the venerable device of having Louis hold the town plan upside-down. Anyway, such issues as these are scarcely fit cause for the conflict in which Grandier is preparing to assist D'Armagnac, and thus to hasten his own downfall.

Philosophically, of course, there is no need for the cause of Grandier's downfall to be a great one—the less its significance, indeed, the greater the stress upon his self-willing of the conflict. As D'Armagnac himself says:

> My dear fellow, we are all romantic. We see our lives being changed by a winged messenger on a black horse. But more often than not it turns out to be a shabby little man, who stumbles across our path. [164]

But *theatrically* the shabby little men who thwart D'Armagnac and who destroy Grandier need to exist in the same street, city, nation—in a play, in short, in the same dimension as their victim. Yet in spite of the epic trappings intended to socialise the "public" play, it's more as if the city and its grubbier inhabitants were gremlins in some private nightmare of Grandier's.

There is one other obvious—over-obvious—linking-device between the "public" and the "private" play. This is the character of the Sewerman, who is at work in his municipal drain as the play opens and at the beginning and end of its second act, for the narrative convenience of Grandier. He is a cross between a confidant and a confessor—a figure universalised by the common human denominator of excrement. At once the common man and the licensed fool, to him alone Grandier can confess his feelings, for, as the priest himself puts it:

> Your debasement has given you an unholy elevation. From your superior position be kind, be wise. Pity me. [173]

The Sewerman doesn't much pity Grandier, but he understands him only too well. He is prone to uncomfortable philosophising about the genital relationship between the sexual and the excretory functions, and thus a personification of the debased physicality which permeates the play. Consider, for example, the careful juxtaposition of the delicate mock-marriage of Grandier and Phillipe, which opens act two, and Grandier's second encounter with the Sewerman—their talk turning to the poisonous sewage pits "at the edge of the town . . . where even your beloved here sends in my buckets". [172]

And so Phillipe, like Caelia, shits? So what? To rub Grandier's mind in the Sewerman's excremental vision seems an oddly irrelevant touch of the Martin Luthers—and the sewage symbolism is never even informed with a subswiftian disgust to make it more than a trite pointer to the shared indignity of humankind. But if the Sewerman's symbolic function as overseer of excremental humanity jars with his role of confidant, he is undeniably, though in isolation, useful as a soliloquy-substitute: and Grandier duly aims his private feelings in his direction for the enlightenment of the audience.

There is, certainly, no other character in the play to whom Grandier might have confided these last thoughts, confessed to him by a man just hanged for theft:

GRANDIER: Manhood led him into the power of the senses. With them he worshipped in total adoration a young girl. But he learnt too quickly. He learnt that only gold can decorate the naked body. And so he stole.

SEWERMAN: And so he hanged.

GRANDIER: He confessed something to me alone. It was not for God to hear. It was a man speaking to a man. He said that when he adorned the girl the metal looked colourless, valueless, against her golden skin. That was repentance. [144]

This is important. The verbal vignette is not only delicately evocative—it also pinpoints Grandier's own dilemma in reconciling the human form transcendent with the human body transubstantiated. But this dilemma has nothing to do with the Sewerman or with his employment—except with his employment as a living apology for Whiting's failure to fit Grandier the man into an environment that can dramatise (not merely verbalise) his physical as well as his metaphysical problem. For just as *The Devils* is really two plays, of which Grandier's is one, so the priest himself is two people:

D'ARMAGNAC: Grandier came to see me this morning. I was having breakfast in the garden. He didn't know that I could observe him as he walked towards me. Vulnerable: smiling. He visibly breathed the air. He stopped to watch the peacocks. He fondled a rose as if it were the secret part of a woman. He laughed with the gardener's child. Then he composed himself, and it was another man who sat down beside me and talked for an hour. Where will this other man climb on his ladder of doubt and laughter?
DE CERISAY: Probably to the highest offices of the church.
D'ARMAGNAC: And the man I saw in the garden? [145]

This is the question that the second, private part of *The Devils* sets out to answer. And it is the much more satisfactory of the "two" plays, this individual tragedy of Grandier's.

In Whiting's earlier works, the impulse towards self-destruction was always strong, often dominant. And here

Grandier's struggle towards the stake is a consciously sought physical redemption for his refusal—or inability—to feel tenderness in physical love. The thirty-five-year-old priest's relations with his women—and in particular with Phillipe, his youngest, most innocent and most loving conquest—are attempts to disguise pure sensuality with a little brief affection, attempts which fail with the purgation of the body or, in Phillipe's case, with its pregnancy. And these declines of Grandier's, from moments of sensual ecstasy into disillusioned harshness, mark him out as that unmistakable tragic figure of Whiting's, the hero flawed by a refusal of responsibility towards his fellows, and so working out his own redemptive destruction.

In Grandier's case, however, this process is for the first time entirely conscious. Consider, for example, this exchange with D'Armagnac:

GRANDIER: All worldly things have a single purpose for a man of my kind. Politics, power, the senses, riches, pride, and authority. I choose them with the same care that you, sir, select a weapon. But my intention is different. I need to turn them against myself.

D'ARMAGNAC: To bring about your end?

GRANDIER: Yes. I have a great need to be united with God. Living has drained the need for life from me. My exercise of the senses has flagged to total exhaustion. I am a dead man, compelled to live.

D'ARMAGNAC: You disgust me. This is a sickness.

GRANDIER: No, sir. It is the meaning and purpose. [184]

Grandier's need to be united with God contrasts ironically with Sister Jeanne's identical desire—the one in repudiation and the other in sublimation of sexuality. D'Armagnac, in reply, asks whether "creating the circumstances for your death" is not as sinful in intention as deliberate self-murder: and this, of course, is a crucial question for Grandier, who is alone among Whiting's tragic figures in professing a religious faith. But, as it happens, circumstances turn to the priest's purpose.

His eventual death is, however, not a redemption but a debasement of the body: he is, in essence, required in the final act to suffer bodily for the purely physical pleasures he has indulged in the first and second. And, sure enough, the brief, anti-climactic scenes which follow Grandier's humiliation by torture stress not the salvation of the spirit but the decay of the flesh. The tragedy is, in this sense, the least satisfying, the least cathartic, that Whiting wrote: even Grandier's hope of redemption proves to be an illusion, and all purpose is reduced to absurdity.

Grandier's affair with Phillipe is his last chance of salvation through physical love—but note the terms in which he elaborates his hopes to the Sewerman:

Hope of coming to God by way of a fellow being. Hope that the path, which taken alone, in awful solitude, is a way of despair, can be enlightened by the love of a woman. I have come to believe that by this simple act of committal, which I have done with my heart, it may be possible to reach God by way of happiness. [172–3]

In *A Walk in the Desert*, this is what Tony called "engaging another person's emotions to prove that you exist". [123] And so Phillipe's pregnancy proves two things: that Grandier's hope "of coming to God by way of a fellow being" was vain because it was selfish, and that, for him, the only remaining commitment is to death. The rejection of Phillipe is not merely of her body and of the unborn child she carries, but of hope in Grandier's own salvation through human kind. He must accept the need to turn "all worldly things . . . against myself", but still he cannot believe that the agency of his fulfilment should be absurd, and, as D'Armagnac prophesies, shabby:

> D'ARMAGNAC: You're in danger.
> GRANDIER: Of death? But surely not by a farce such as the convent's putting on. Come, sir, death must be more magnificent, more significant for a man of my kind. [176]

Here, for the first time, Whiting is about to confront one of his heroes with the full existential horror of absurdity. Those of his earlier characters whose self-destruction had been accomplished were enacting a meaningful redemption: those brought face to face with their own insignificance were left with the knowledge of it to linger out their lives. But in *The Devils* time and circumstance give a tragic twist to what could, a few hundred years later, easily have been just another sexual farce.

Grandier has to be further humbled. In the senses he sought self-destruction, and in their rejection he prays to God to be able to give himself "into the hands of the world secure in the faith of Your mysterious ways", [187] rejoicing in the expectation of death. But then, in his final meeting with the Sewerman, he describes how he has now re-created God in his own image, in an epiphanic confrontation with the raw-materials of existence:

> I created Him from the light and the air, from the dust of the road, from the sweat of my hands, from gold, from filth, from the memory of women's faces, from great

rivers, from children, from the works of man, from the past, the present, the future, and the unknown. I caused Him to be from fear and despair. I gathered in everything from this mighty act, all I have known, seen and experienced. My sin, my presumption, my vanity, my love, my hate, my lust. And last I gave myself and so made God. And He was magnificent. For He is all these things. [199]

Sadly, Whiting is at his weakest as a theologian. Grandier's pantheistic heresy is neither original nor very remarkably expressed: and from this moment, almost at the close of the second act, the working-out of his fate, and the putting to the test of his new but hard-won faith, become obscured.

The grotesque physicality which has up to this point been no more than a *symptom* of Grandier's suffering now becomes dominant: "it is the meaning and purpose" indeed. The sequential action has effectively been brought to a close with the priest's arrest at the end of the second act: and so the last act becomes an exploration in close-up of the nature of pain itself, in which unalloyed spasms of unendurable agony are at first horrifying, but quickly modify themselves into a dramatic convention for pain as the law of diminishing returns begins to operate. Before his torture Grandier has pleaded: "There are two things a man should never be asked to do in front of other men. Perform with a woman, and suffer pain." [215] And one becomes uncomfortably aware that the mere performance of suffering before a theatre audience is as inadequate a dramatic statement of pain as would Grandier's mere performance with Phillipe have been of full sensuality.

At the beginning of *The Devils* a corpse hangs from the gallows and the Sewerman works in his drain—busy allegorising the sex act in terms of a man finding "comfort in his wife's conduit". [143] Soon the surgeon and the chemist are busy speculating over a human head, which they look forward to dissecting, and upon a foetus the surgeon has just aborted. [146–7] Father Barré talks of the "black slime" on the forehead of a supposedly possessed girl, [151] and describes an evil spirit "speaking through the umbilicus of a child". [152] A stuffed crocodile and "bottles which hold malformed creatures" decorate the scenes in the pharmacy, [153] where Grandier later accuses Adam and Mannoury of "distilling bile in retorts". [166] This harping on physical ugliness or corruption either counterpoints or juxtaposes every episode in the first act: even Grandier's pledge of love for Phillipe is sandwiched between two scenes in the pharmacy, and the act ends with hunchbacked Jeanne's first encounter with the babbling Barré.

This relentless pressure of grotesqueries, visual and verbal, is relaxed only as the demonic circus got up by the nuns begins to dominate the action during the second act: and the third is taken up entirely with Grandier's humiliation of the body. The audience's parting glimpse of the priest is of his first and only physical encounter with Sister Jeanne —a shattered body confronting a deformed one. And their single exchange does, at last, transcend the physical:

> JEANNE: Thev always spoke of your beauty. Now I see it with my own eyes and I know it to be true.
> GRANDIER: Look at this thing which I am, and learn the meaning of love. [217]

But it is too late to learn—for Jeanne, for Grandier, and for the audience.

The conflict in the last act has been between pain and Grandier's self-created conception of God. "There will be pain. It will kill God." [202] This is Grandier's fear: and his hope, taught him by the visit of the gentle, simple Father Ambrose, is that "pain, convulsion and disgust" can themselves be offered up to God—the sinner who has "lived by the senses" letting God reveal himself in the only way he can understand.

AMBROSE: It is all any of us can do. We live a little while, and in that little while we sin. We go to Him as we can. All is forgiven.

GRANDIER: Yes, I am His child. It is true. Let Him take me as I am. So there is meaning. There is meaning, after all. I am a sinful man and I can be accepted. It is not nothing going to nothing. It is sin going to forgiveness. It is a human creature going to love. [204–5]

This is a sudden and not altogether satisfactory change of direction. The terms of the dialectics here are as inadequately prepared for as the presence of Father Ambrose himself: the philosophy is attractive, but its attraction is that of *A Penny for a Song*. Grandier lives in his sensuality, but not in his salvation: and the scenes of riot and of horrific abandon which follow the confrontation between Grandier and Sister Jeanne heighten this impression even after his death. [218–19]

It is, then, in its dialectics that the play is least satisfactory —the more so since its ostensibly epic foundations need to be shored up by argument, so that one cannot here rely simply on the allusive or tangential insights of Whiting's earlier works. For example: the possessed nuns, though their antics enliven the second act, are, psychologically and dramatically, "givens"—capering about like Middleton's madmen in *The Changeling*, and understood little better. Such explanations of their behaviour as are offered are of the tritest. And Grandier's own feeling that "they give themselves to God, but something remains that cries out to be given to Man" [177] is apparently shared by the playwright as he shapes the nuns' early actions. But the stress upon their manipulative control over their behaviour is gradually increased, until—transformed into menagerie freaks planning their own itinerary—they are shown revelling in their new-found notoriety in two of the most uncomfortable scenes in the play. [195–6 and 205–6] And yet, after De Condé's revelation of their rather too perfect self-control, [193–4] Whiting has Sister Jeanne converse with Leviathan, the spirit allegedly possessing her, and ends his scene with the pair laughing together. The suggestion is maybe of meddlers with devilish things hoist on their own petards: but the hint of such a moral complication is *dramatically* an over-simplification.

Perhaps Whiting could not make up his own mind about the nature of the nuns' possession—as he certainly never made it up about their relative importance in the action, which veers erratically from the dominant to the incidental. It may be worth noting that Whiting seems most alert to his nuns as practical jokers—and just as they are betrayed by De Condé's trick, so Sister Jeanne's most elaborate defence of their deception centres upon practical joking. Her speech needs quoting in full, for although Jeanne is a relatively minor character in *The Devils*—probably to the play's dialectical detriment—here she comes far closer to Whiting's earlier tragic figures than Grandier himself ever does. "Have we mocked God?" she is asked by Sister Louise. "It was not the intention," Jeanne replies:

But to make a mockery of man. That's a different matter. For what a splendid creature he makes to be fooled. He might have been created for no other purpose. With his head in the air, besotted with his own achievement, he asks to be tripped. Deep in the invention of mumbo-jumbo to justify his existence, he is deaf to laughter. With no eyes for anything but himself, he's blind to the gesture of ridicule made in front of his face.

So, drunk, deaf and blind, he goes on. The perfect subject for the practical joke. And that, my sisters, is where the children of misfortune—like me—play a part. We do not mock our beloved Father in Heaven. Our laughter is kept for His wretched and sinful children who get above their station, and come to believe they have some other purpose in this world than to die.

After the delusions of power come the delusions of love. When men cannot destroy they start to believe they can be saved by creeping into a fellow human being. And so perpetuating themselves. Love me, they say over and over again, love me. Cherish me. Defend me. Save me. They say it to their wives, their whores, their children, and some to the whole human race. Never to God. These are probably the most ridiculous of all, and most worthy of derision. For they do not understand the glory of mortality, the purpose of man: loneliness and death
[186]

This is an inconclusive note on which to leave *The Devils*: but then *The Devils* is a highly inconclusive play. And there could be no more appropriate point from which to return, following the next chapter on Whiting's critical work, to some more general remarks about his plays. Thus, the thread of Sister Jeanne's speech will best be taken up in my concluding chapter: for it is a thread that can be traced through each of Whiting's plays, and which links even the stupid provincial grocer of *Conditions of Agreement* with the proud and worldly priest of *The Devils*. Both were the victims of practical jokes played by "the children of misfortune".

5

Doubts and Reassurance

The Art of the Dramatist and
John Whiting on Theatre

WHITING'S EDITOR, Ronald Hayman, has collected into
posthumous printed form a certain amount of material that,
fascinating though it is for the fanatical admirer of Whiting's
work, might well have been left to its elusiveness in little
magazines and private archives by the dramatist himself.
Work which was incomplete at his death falls, of course, into
rather a different category: but those fragments of his "last"
play *The Nomads* which appear in the *Collected Plays* can
scarcely do more than tantalise—and certainly cannot be
judged adequately by the critic, none of whose business is it
to offer unsolicited comments on the work-in-progress on a
writer's desk. For this reason, I have not considered in the
present study either *The Nomads* or the earlier, unfinished
Noman—which (although it too is included in the *Collected
Plays*) "couldn't ever work" in Whiting's own opinion. That
it is also "boring beyond words" is perhaps an over-harsh
judgement, but on a work Whiting chose to abandon it is
better that it should be the playwright's than my own.[36]

Of the ragbag of stories, articles, lectures and reviews
which Hayman has gathered together in the volume *The
Art of the Dramatist*, I shall, therefore, discuss in this chapter
only those left by Whiting in at least a tentatively finished

state. Such a qualification canonises not only the most interesting material in *The Art of the Dramatist* but also the columns
of theatre criticism Whiting contributed to the *London
Magazine* in 1961 and 1962, and which were assembled after
his death into the slim but stimulating volume called simply
John Whiting on Theatre. From these two collections one can
begin to deduce the approach to dramaturgy which formed
the theoretical basis of Whiting's playwriting—besides
glimpsing, in the early non-dramatic prose, the origins of
some of his preoccupations in the plays.

   Although an unpublished novel, *Not a Foot of Land*, exists,[37]
Whiting did not experiment widely outside the dramatic
form, and the handful of pieces of "creative" writing in
The Art of the Dramatist are recognisably brief detours by a
born dramatist rather than considerable works in their own
right. They share a bald, almost phlegmatic narrative style
—as if Whiting was keeping a distance between himself and
his words, as he so often distanced his characters from their
own more self-descriptive dialogue—and an appropriately
abrupt manner of observation, which in its juxtapositions
often creates from the outwardly commonplace something
approaching the surreal. The tone of the first vignette—for
it is imagistically that all these early pieces impress—is
characteristic. Called "Fragment of a Novel", it is an
uncensorious, almost clinically remote analysis of a young
girl's pathological lethargy (and of how others respond to it)
which, backtracking in time, touches also upon its origins
in early childhood. Written in 1947, the piece foreshadows
several of the familiar themes of the plays—the child left a
spiritual cripple by an illness as purposeless as her mother's
subsequent death in a car accident, and the father retreating
for solace to the surroundings of his own childhood, a time
when one responds to affection "with an avid, grasping . . .

desire for an even greater excess''. [21] The fragment opens as the nineteen-year-old girl wakes from the afternoon sleep that is her attempt to "withdraw as far as possible—without dying" from the trivial demands of her waking life. [16] Pausing to retrace the course of her enigmatically cheerless infancy, the narrative breaks off just as the girl's bereaved father meets the woman who is to become her stepmother—and who, at the beginning of the story, has commented acidly upon the stupidity of the supposedly sleeping girl.

This elliptic beginning—seemingly anticipating a full-length study into adulthood of a neurosis rooted in infancy—makes an appropriate curtain-raiser to *Conditions of Agreement*, just as the next surviving story, "The Honour of the Fire Brigade", written in 1948, does to *A Penny for a Song*. Its hero, the narrator's grandfather, a rural worthy who takes his supposed sinecure as captain of the local fire brigade with disconcerting seriousness, is recognisably from the same mould as Lamprett Bellboys—though his enthusiasm for fire engines is updated a hundred years, and the excuse for the climactic pyrotechnics is not the Napoleonic Wars but the Coronation of King George V. Many touches, though, are identical—there is even talk of "a demolition charge for preventing the spread of fire". [27] And the tone as well as the theme is comparable—the delightful *openness* of the vision unsoured. Here, one is tempted into acquiescence in the pleasantly absurd, not resignation before the bitterly inconsequent: and, within the limits of its own anecdotal form, "The Honour of the Fire Brigade" is quite simply—its simplicity is of its essence—very funny.

"A Valediction", written in 1949, returns to the terrors of childhood, to the death of a parent and its consequences—and to a flatter, dispassionate narrative style:

E

"Edward," she said, "are you good?"

"Yes," the boy answered, directly. [31]

Edward, his father dying as the story opens, looks out enviously from a stately-home—made more sombre by mourning—as a circus procession passes by. On the evening of his father's funeral, the boy escapes, innocently cunning, to the fair. He meets the three children of a poor artist on the way, visits the big top itself, where the final procession of performers seems a grotesque parody of that morning's march behind the gun carriage—and, making his reluctant but exhilarated way home, sees the clowns "speaking together, nodding, smiling". He stops, unnoticed, to observe:

> The tallest clown laughed aloud and, stretching up, peeled away his bald pate, and with it came the tiny hat. The smallest clown yawned and his monstrous nose dropped away. The third clown tore off his plaster ears and from all three the familiar, false hilarity of their faces was gone.
>
> Edward stared in horror at this dreadful decomposition and then, as the storm of grief and knowledge swept through him, stretched out his hands.
>
> "Dead men! Dead men!" he screamed.

And he runs back in terror to "the domed building standing on the hill". [39] This incident is, of course, particularly compelling for any student of Whiting's early work who is familiar with the fascination clowns and circuses exerted over him: but "A Valediction" has a rightness and completeness quite independent of its associations, and through its blunt, literal idiom finds exactly the tone its curious theme requires.

There is a similar quality about the revealingly titled "Child's Play", also written in 1949. Here, another small boy is gradually won over to a liking for the man his mother intends to marry—not by the prospective stepfather's own earnest efforts, but by the sight of the grown man tumbling, gracefully but accidentally, into a snowdrift. Although this strikes yet again a note nearly of cruelty, certainly of the absurd, there is in this story a mutual receptivity between boy and adult not often found—outside *A Penny for a Song*— in Whiting's portrayals of such relationships. This is a slighter, almost anecdotal piece—really adding up to little more than an ironic reflection upon the prospective step-father's theory that children "are given to judgement by exterior appearances" [40]—but one notes nevertheless that the boy intends to "go into a circus as a clown", [44] and that his heart is finally won by a clown-like pratfall. And, for what it's worth, his christian name, like Bembo's, is Peter.

A deeply-felt but oddly uninspiring meditation upon Good Friday, "The Image of Majesty", written in 1962, and an undated, embittered attack on the commonplaces of the twentieth century and its bureaucratic evasions, "Scenario for a Film"—which fails to transcend the triteness of its subject-matter—are the only other pieces of creative prose preserved in *The Art of the Dramatist*. Both suggest, as do the short stories themselves, how firmly harnessed to the dramatic impulse Whiting really was—the "Scenario" specifying that it is to be "spoken without any great emphasis", as if Whiting couldn't resist stage-directing even the narrative poetry he here employed. [62] Verifying this impression of a total commitment to the theatre, the whole of his considerable output of critical writing was itself devoted to the drama— constituting the fullest body of theory and comment on the subject left by any major British playwright since Shaw.

But if Whiting had the instinctive feeling for dramatic craftsmanship his early proficiency seems to proclaim, he adapted to the rather different demands of the craft of criticism less readily. Magnificently transcending the conventions of his times in the matter of *writing* plays, he could be curiously constricted by them when criticising the work of others, or theorising about his own. And, unlike Shaw, he sometimes found it hard to see a play from front-of-house—his actor's training, perhaps, provoking him into comments extraneous to the experience of the audience. In any case, it will be convenient to separate his more discursive writings about the theatre from his reviews of plays in performance—a distinction which makes chronological sense besides, because the latter were written mainly in the two or three years before his death, after a period of comparative inactivity as a critical theorist.

The earliest of all these pieces, "Writing for Actors" (1952), formulates with an air of discovery a number of not very original dicta concerning the relationship between writer, director and actors within the unquestioned confines of the "well-made" three-act format. Sometimes, it's true, the unexceptionable is expressed with the pleasing freshness of individual illumination:

> The basic, the unalterable factor of drama is the moment "when"; the moment of happening which is contained in the action. The dramatist must concern himself with this moment of action and not leave it, as so often happens, to be imposed by the director or players. In other words, the dramatist must create what is done and *when*, and not only the words to be spoken. [107]

> Formal structure is the poetry of drama. Given this, anything is possible to the actor. From it he can build in a

disciplined and poetic way. Without it he will retreat into naturalism, and instead of acting he will behave. [109]

The piece amounts to a none-too-hopeful plea for the theatre "to become an art in its own right", so that "it may be possible to talk about the modern play in the same sense as modern music and modern painting". [109–10] Yet in "A Conversation", originally published in 1953, Whiting seems to doubt whether the play form may not "have reached its ultimate point of development a long time ago", [116] and, returning to the problem of "writing for actors", he comes up with some very strange conclusions indeed.

Cast in a laconic dialogue form, this piece makes its distinction between the "literary' and the "theatrical" play well enough on a theoretical level, but seems, in retrospect, decidedly near-sighted in its claim that Rattigan's *Deep Blue Sea* and Graham Greene's *The Living Room* "yield everything to be asked of a performance in a theatre". [113] To this Whiting's antagonist is made to retort that "very soon the theatre will break through to something new and exciting"—a claim on which the Whiting *persona* pours scorn. [116] Yet only three years were to pass before *Look Back in Anger* achieved a breakthrough of sorts, and plays which (whatever their ultimate value may prove to be) were worth a dozen *Deep Blue Seas* did reach the living stage.

In the following year, Whiting ghosted a letter of rebuke on behalf of his antagonist, who declares himself "shocked that you thought fit to publish our conversation".[38] But it sheds little further light on Whiting's own views, beyond confirming which of the two characters in the earlier dialogue he had intended to represent them. "To the Playguehouse to See the Smirching of Venus" (1956)—a title taken from *Finnegan's Wake*—does, however, take up a subject which

Whiting was to explore in several essays of this period: the need for a new notation for dramatic speech and action. This had been briefly touched on in "Writing for Actors", in his anticipation of "a script which is only comprehensible to the theatre worker and remains nonsense to the layman". [108] Curiously, however, stage directions, in the earlier piece described as "the author's first means of communication with his actors", [107] are now regarded merely as "the crutches of play-writing". The real "extension of the play form"

> must be in the language. Then it may well be possible to use dramatic devices, such as a form of soliloquy, which have fallen into disuse. Also we may find, as is rightly urged on us by Kenneth Tynan, a way of speech which will strike on the ear with the clarity never born of gentility. That style as it develops will, I feel, have less and less to do with "literature" as we understand it today. [123]

Here the prophecy is more specific, and nearer, indeed, to the truth—revealing an insight that recurs, for example, in Whiting's subsequent recognition of the affinity between his own work and *Waiting for Godot*. This affinity is not of a literary kind, he claims, but to do with a "disciplined form of notation, which yet allows for flexible interpretation". [126] Yet "From a Notebook"—the first of three such assortments of epigrams, anecdotes and vivid images, published in 1956—contains, besides this illuminating comparison, a pervasive pessimism and even an occasional note of pettishness. In many ways these collections of public memorabilia are the most revealing of Whiting's non-dramatic writings—making one regret, incidentally, that he was no diarist. Yet *what* they reveal is a temperamental uncertainty towards his public, a tendency towards introspective self-mockery, and a certain ambivalence towards his art. Here is one entry in its entirety:

I am getting old. I found myself the other day wishing that there could be a play unexpectedly performed in London, brilliant, successful, the critics enraptured, and written by someone about twenty years old. Is this too much to hope for nowadays? Or is the theatre getting old? Such things are in the past. As a critic said to me the other day when speaking of my plays, "Cheer up, nobody writes anything much—especially for the theatre—until they're past forty." Consolation? No. [128]

One has to remind oneself, again, that this was written in 1956, the year of *Look Back in Anger*. Yet so much of Whiting's prose has the feeling one senses here of being wrong for all the right reasons—in this same "Notebook", for example, there is an epitaph for the provincial theatre, cruelly exact in analysis, but written at a time when it, too, was on the brink of a renaissance.

Most of the other jottings share a reflective sadness—even the sadness of not feeling "angry or sad enough to write a new play". [131] And this is carried over into the next piece reprinted in *The Art of the Dramatist*, "The Toll of Talent in a Timid Theatre"—originally written, also in 1956, for *Encore*. Here, the mood even descends into a rare self-pity in this carefully impersonal reflection upon

the young playwrights, the anonymous men and women of English literature. They are eternally promising, everlastingly young: never fulfilled, alas, until their wits are rocking, in exile, aged, finished, and fair game for the patronising article. No other branch of literature seems to suffer casualties as does play-writing. The loss of life is negligible, but the loss of talent is enormous. Again, the English don't actually kill playwrights: they just say, "Oh, I thought he was dead." [132–3]

But there is, of course, more than a wry reflection on Whiting's own treatment here: there is the insight of a dramatist one of whose earliest plays portrayed a writer honoured only "in exile, aged, finished"—as was Paul Southman, whom most people, indeed, thought dead.

Though denying that there is any such thing as an "actor's theatre" or a "director's theatre", and asserting that "the theatre belongs to the writer and always has", [133–4] Whiting admits in the undated piece "A Man of the Theatre" that "the playwright in England has become the black sheep of literature". Prophetically, he notes the emergence in the theatre of "a barely repressed feeling of resentment that the genesis of a play is literary. I mean, to do with words". [135] Unfortunately, as in so much of Whiting's theoretical writing of the 'fifties, the illuminating idea remains unexplored, the argument not followed through. Too many of these essays amble on discursively and often—from one to the next—contradictorily. In "A Man of the Theatre", for example, Whiting's traditional literary position is not really compatible with his earlier hope for "clarity never born of gentility". Then, in "The Writers' Theatre", also published in 1956, he concedes that the "actors' theatre . . . is the theatre in England today", a fact of life he had been reluctant to admit in the earlier essay.

In "The Writers' Theatre" Whiting does, however, elaborate his earlier concern for the dilution of the literary content of theatre:

A sad parting of the ways has occurred between the playwright and his interpreters. To the writer, drama is a basic form: the theatre is a toy, an ingenious piece of machinery. It exists for the interpretation of plays. To many actors and directors it has become a thing in itself, tiresomely dependent on some form of content. Actors have not yet reached a point in their art where they can merely be. They still have to do something. [140–1]

Whiting does not view this state of affairs in what might— with the hindsight of fifteen more years, which have seen happenings happen and texts torn to shreds lest the drama-tist's words should get in the way of the actors "merely being" —seem a prophetic vision of the mentality of an increasingly introverted theatrical profession. Rather, he blames the critics for setting standards which have led to the stultifica-tion of dramatic form—and then wonders, as he had earlier in "A Conversation", whether the form itself may be

not capable of much development. The ideas, yes: the form, no. And the form, as we see, is all important.

The rise of the curtain. The point of entry into the action. The argument. The development. The conclusion. The whole formal conjuring trick. Everything must be subordinated to the illusion. If it is not, there is a feeling of unease, of embarrassment. And the question becomes, Are we in a theatre? When the answer is definitely, yes, the reaction is immediate flight. A trick has been performed, but it was not the trick that was expected, or, more accurately, the trick that has come to be expected. The audience must be taken out of themselves, their attention must never be turned in upon themselves. Or so it seems. That is what an audience wants. [142–3]

And this takes us to the heart of the paradox that was Whiting's relationship with his audience—and which threatened to undermine his relationship with his art. He assumed that "what an audience wants" is escapist trivia, and to be "taken out of themselves", yet he not only accepted but championed an elitist conception of art that would prevent his plays from reaching any other audience.

Thus, just one paragraph before reaching the conclusions quoted above, he declared that it was "a mistake to see the theatre as a popular art. . . . The play must now be directed towards a specialised audience." [142] And so the argument seems to run: the dramatist must write plays for a specialised elite, which at present has certain rather unworthy expectations. These must unfortunately be satisfied, yet, because they permit no challenge to be made to an audience's sensibilities —whereas it is the purpose of art precisely to raise doubts— the artist must either compromise or perish. And the *only* reason Whiting advances for the theatre's inability to become once more a popular art—conceding that "it may have been fifty years ago"—is that "new mediums have changed all that". [142]

What perverse fatalism was it, then, that prompted him to address plays to audiences he acknowledged didn't even *want* to understand them? Recalling Martin Esslin's story of the prisoners of San Quentin who instantly recognised their own predicament in that of *Waiting for Godot*, one wonders whether an audience—say—of post-war central European refugees might not have responded to *Saint's Day* where one of West End first-nighters was merely baffled or enraged. Yet it is for these latter that Whiting continued to write, and these from whom he expected his elite to emerge. Instead, they spat in his face.

And so to "The Art of the Dramatist", the text of the lecture which, both from its length and the evident care that went into its preparation, can be considered virtually a definitive statement of Whiting's position.[39] One notes, too, that his output of theoretical essays reached a peak in 1956, the year before the lecture was delivered, thereafter to trail away as his critical interests turned more and more to the work of other playwrights—and, the unkind observer might add, as the work of other playwrights increasingly merited such attention, in consequence making his personal, pessimistic theory of dramatic art rather less tenable.

Briefly, Whiting's view in "The Art of the Dramatist" is that the arts, in spite of an organisational set-up dedicated to concealing the fact, are dying. They are dying because "a work of art is the statement of one man", [82] whereas what is now demanded is "the communal voice" supposedly representing "the great mass of people" educated by public library reading to a superficial awareness of art. But the educational propagandists did not realise one of the consequences of their philanthropy—"that the status of art would be changed". [85] By this, however, Whiting is not referring to the even then discernible tendency of critics and others to capitulate before the onslaught of so-called "pop" culture, but to the genuine attempts of young writers to reflect the reality of working-class life in their work— sometimes, confessedly, with propaganda aforethought, but usually for no better or worse reason than that it was the reality with which they were most richly acquainted, or which they felt others had not fully explored. Rather, claims Whiting, such writers insist that plays about contemporary world problems must also "be set *in* a concentration camp, *beneath* an imminent explosion, or *in* a new town". [86] Ignoring the negligible number of plays set in concentration camps or beneath imminent explosions, one notes the assumption, typical of Whiting's thinking, that living in a new town is somehow a comparably traumatic experience, and the stuff of which mere journalism rather than drama must be made.

Whiting himself admitted that he had "no idea how playwrights go about their job. Except one. And that is myself." [87] And *he himself* did not, of course, write plays of social comment or documentary realism—although, as he remarks, all writers have been "touched by these things . . . and if the play is anything of a serious work it must be shadowed by them". [87] *For him*, then, the genesis of a play lies not in a consciously wrought theme, or a thesis to be illustrated, but in a trivial, even inconsequential incident:

> It may be seeing some girl in a restaurant: it may be getting frighteningly lost in a foreign city: or getting drunk. It may be very important, something to change the whole life, such as the death of a friend. Anyway, it happens and the lost idea recurs. It comes back. Subtly invested with a significance it never had before. The impulse at once is to translate it into an attempted work of art. In my case, a play. The intellectual notion and the happening in life breed. Sometimes in an odd way. The pretty girl who smiled in the bookshop may give birth to a political tragedy. The dying friend to farce. [89]

From this germ evolves what Whiting calls the "thing given": the moment *in the action* which defines it, and towards or from which, structurally, the rest of the play works—what he had earlier called "the moment 'when' ". The play needs, additionally, a place—for Whiting, "a real place, a room, a garden, what we call a naturalistic setting". It needs a time. And (that this should come so low in the

order of priorities is interesting) it needs characters, though it
would be wrong to believe that

> the characters of a play *are* the play, that they make up the
> play. It is an easy mistake to make, because the people in a
> play are the most easily and immediately comprehensible
> factor. But, in fact, the play is formed by circumstances
> reacting on character. [93]

It is from all these elements—theme, place, time, people—
that the play's structure takes shape, and "every structure
will depend on the diversity of these elements". [95]

Yet even when the words which clothe that skeletal form
are on paper, there remain all the differences of class, usage
and generation which erect barriers to their understanding:

> Today the most acceptable form of language in the
> theatre it would seem is the direct unornamented speech of
> everyday life. Acceptable to an audience, I mean. But
> what is this direct unornamented speech? Pick up a
> conversation in the street and it may go something like
> this:
> "Now look here I said I'm not having this I said and so
> he says What and I says I'm not having it, I'm telling
> you I says up and down the stairs you were four times this
> morning telling him I was up and down I says in your
> boots with little Else trying to sleep oh I told him."
> No, the direct unornamented speech of the theatre
> must be as artificial as any form. [97]

If anything, of course, Whiting's exercise in eavesdropping
on unornamented speech suggests just the opposite—as, in his
laconic review of the lecture, Kenneth Tynan noticed:

How repetitive! he implied. How drab and dull! It was in fact infectiously and rivetingly alive. One longed to hear more. I realised then, with a sense of wild frustration, that Mr Whiting was a born playwright determined at all costs not to be a playwright at all.

Earlier in this review, Tynan had pinpointed a funda-mental objection to the lecture as a whole—not that it out-lines, quite persuasively, one man's method of playwriting at the expense of everyman's, but that it actually refuses to recognise the limitations (once recognised, the potential advantages) of the medium itself:

I began to wonder whether we were talking about the theatre at all. Were we not rather talking about poetry or the novel, private arts intended to be sampled by one person at a time? Had we not somehow strayed from the drama, a public art which must be addressed to hundreds of people at the same time? Somewhere in Mr Whiting's imagination there glows a vision of an ideal theatre where the playwright is freed from the necessity of attracting customers, where his fastidious cadences are not tainted by exposure to rank plebeian breath. It is a theatre with-out an audience. And it exists—again in Mr Whiting's imagination—as a gesture of defiance against those other, equally mythical London theatres where socially signi-ficant plays about concentration camps are constantly being staged to the vociferous approval of "the masses".

"Anyone not a playwright," Tynan hazards parenthetically, "belongs, in Mr Whiting's mind, to the masses."[40]

Now of course Whiting was aware of the theatre as a "public art", and his "fastidious cadences" were shaped, almost scored, to be spoken by actors. But Tynan's criticisms, for all their flippancy, contain a kernel of truth. Whiting *was* a playwright in spite of himself, practising an art that was private in so far as it was addressed to an *audience* that existed only in his own mind. The people who actually came to see his plays—or who chose to stay away from them—fell lamentably short of his ideal, although, paradoxically, a "popular audience" such as he affected to despise might have been less hidebound in its expectations and so have proved more receptive. In such a way, at least, the shock tactics of the early "social" dramatists whose work he condemned had the side-effect of clearing the ground for a better understanding in the theatre of Whiting himself— and he even concluded his lecture in ironic anticipation of this:

> People are too wise now, and the young too charmingly cynical for artists to go on in the old way.
>
> The remedy lies with one man, because all the buildings, the managerial offices, the impresarios, the directors, the designers, the actors, the musicians, the men who move the scenery, the people who take the money at the box office, the critics and the gossip writers, depend on that one man. The dramatist, alone in his room, happily or miserably, with ease or with difficulty, cynically or wholeheartedly, writing a play. The dramatist practising his art. [100]

For us the irony here lies not only in our knowledge that the lonely figure of Whiting, gloomily diagnosing the ills of the drama, had in his own works given us clues to the remedy, but in an uncomfortable awareness that it was those writers he felt to be at best poorly qualified and at worst quacks who began to complete the cure.

That Whiting *did* come to acknowledge this, though never directly—indeed, he continued to snipe at the Royal Court dramatists until his death—is at least implicit in the notices he wrote for the *London Magazine* in 1961 and 1962, collected into the volume *John Whiting on Theatre*. Interestingly, that he should become a dramatic critic at all was in defiance of his own earlier belief that the dramatist "is never allowed the amusement of reviewing. Dramatic criticism, like play-writing, is considered to be a closed shop." [136] But well before his act of shop-breaking, Whiting had evidently begun to lose interest in the theoretical side of his work, and the few pieces which followed "The Art of the Dramatist"—notably "At Ease in a Bright Red Tie", written for *Encore* in 1959[41]—are already more concerned with passing judgement on his fellow playwrights than with defining his own position—although, necessarily, the latter often emerges indirectly from the former.

The first of these reprinted reviews, "Inside the Asylum", asks whether the British theatre has really crossed the boundaries which have traditionally cut it off from the people, and decides that it hasn't:

So we have this curious situation. Dramatists writing plays, actors performing them, and critics reviewing them: all being done in a private world. . . . These people believe themselves to be stridently engaged in life. Reality —these words!—is the new myth-making substance. Fix it with absolute accuracy and it will transcend itself to the point of revelation. That is what many people in the theatre believe. So do madmen. [11]

Yet much of what Whiting wrote in the following year or so was to challenge this conclusion. In Sartre's *Altona*, as produced at the Royal Court, he detected a "new romantic-ism" of poeticised brutality, but at the same time a play "very frightening in its statement of despair".

We act, and by acting we commit the crime. We are aware of our monstrous indiscretion. We long for judgement and punishment. We face our judges and at once the position is absurd, for they are as guilty as we are. We implore their condemnation, but they will not speak. They are aware of the counter-charge. So accused and accuser stand face to face in impotent silence, both asking for conviction from an authority which does not exist. [15]

And something of the quintessence of the writer is caught in the strange reassurance Whiting goes on to draw: "There is comfort in the understanding that we are all capable of great crimes. For if it is not so then we are innocent, and so lost." [16]

Similarly, it is not so much the praise or blame Whiting apportions in his other notices as the evidence he selects in support that throws light on his own feelings. Commending the innovatory political revue, *Beyond the Fringe*, he will maintain that "laughter is now a serious business", because

Dr Verwoerd speaks of good neighbourliness, President Kennedy of being threatened by Cuba, Eichmann of how his auntie came of really quite nice people. We believe our ears. We fall about. [22]

But our laughter, he continues, no longer has much to do with happiness. Or, of the climax of Wesker's *The Kitchen*, he will write:

The workers . . . stand silent and shocked as the bloody figure of the German cook is taken away. Social man, and the servers of social man, are at a standstill both in awe of, and homage to, the agony of an individual. [31]

Now this, of course, is only one of several ways of interpreting Wesker's ending—it would be as permissible to suggest that "individual" selfishness and greed have reduced a would-be "social" creature to his lonely agony—but it is revealing that it is the perspective Whiting should choose.

His notice of Osborne's *Luther* is curiously evasive—a non-review of what he regarded, in its unfaithfulness to the author's intentions, as a non-production. He praises Kenneth Tynan in a review of his collected criticism, *Curtains*—tantalisingly abstaining from comment on the pen portrait of himself in that volume, though pertinently returning the compliment. Yet, in his very next notice—of Christopher Fry's disappointing, almost formulaic verse-drama about Becket, *Curtmantle*, he is able to ignore the new theatrical spirit Tynan chronicled, in order to lavish praise on those points of Fry's work at which it most nearly touches his own —its bald, muted treatment of a nevertheless extraordinary central character, and its charting of the consequences of "the most casual and thoughtless act" in a man's life. [54] And it is here that he digresses into an attack on a more recent column of Tynan's headed "No Time for Tragedy",[42] asserting that Arthur Miller's Willy Loman did not, as Tynan claimed, die because the company he worked for had no pensions scheme, but "as we shall all die, because he was a foolish, weak man". [59] For "the tragedy of men is that they are men". [60]

Of a book on method acting by Charles Marowitz, improbably included in a series of amateur theatre handbooks, he observes: "This makes for hilarious possibilities in the old church hall on a Saturday night." [65] Of Brian Rix's succession of Whitehall farces: "We have, thank God, the silly theatre. Let us cherish it." [73–4] And of Noel Coward's doomed attempts to fly in the face of democracy: "He did something which has proved disastrous to him as an artist of the theatre: he raised his voice." [104] As a critic, Whiting never made the same mistake, nor set limits to the kinds of theatre he was prepared to treat seriously. But often his angle of vision narrows until one is almost deceived into thinking that the subject is one of his own plays. Thus, of *The Cherry Orchard*:

Chekhov himself described it as being "not a drama but a comedy; in places almost a farce". But if we say, as the dictionary does, that comedy is "a branch of drama concerned with ordinary persons and employing familiar language", and that farce is "an absurdly futile proceeding, a pretence, a mockery", we almost exactly describe *The Cherry Orchard*. [78]

Or *Conditions of Agreement*. Or *The Gates of Summer*. And, finally, consider this view of Brecht's *Caucasian Chalk Circle*, taken from one of the last reviews Whiting wrote—a strikingly favourable one of William Gaskill's production at the Aldwych:

The dialectic of the play has some strange conclusions considering its origin. The children belong to those who are motherly; the land to those who will water it and make it fruitful. In short, it is a play about human love. And, curious for our time, love not confused by sex. The implications contained in the play about the law of possession are also very disturbing. It may be, and we can only hope it will be, fully understood in about five hundred years' time. [95]

This exemplifies both the qualities and limitations of Whiting's criticism of the live theatre: an ability to seize on and define a play's less readily apparent qualities, which is limited by his inclination to transform it into the work he would have written himself—and, consequently, also by the tendency to over-simplify which is apparent in his comments on his own plays. *A Penny for a Song*, remember, was "simply" about Christian charity. And now *The Caucasian Chalk Circle* is "a play about human love". Yet arguably this is among the most fruitful ways of engaging a critical response—the ability to provoke the interested reaction, "yes, but . . ." It is, after all, also one's first response to the ambiguities and subtleties of the plays themselves.

CONCLUSION

Conclusion

"'LIKE SHAKESPEARE'S, his plays will return to us, glittering." Thus wrote Whiting during the period after Bernard Shaw's death when that dramatist was, predictably but briefly, out of fashion.[43] Whiting's work, too, must surely return to us—specifically, must return to the theatre, for it has grown slowly but steadily in literary-critical esteem. But it will return not so much glittering as rich and sombre—for no writer could have been less like Shaw, whether in his rhetoric, his feelings towards his audience, or his attitude towards his art. Indeed, Whiting not only repudiated the didacticism in which Shaw delighted, but claimed that "some of the best art teaches nothing, and can do irreparable harm, if not actually deprave".[44] Tantalisingly, he did not particularise. Could he, perhaps, have been contemplating the effects of his own plays? The repudiation of society and the course of self-destruction plotted in *Saint's Day*? The ironic nihilism of *Marching Song*? The bitter, arguably life-denying comedies of *Conditions of Agreement* and *The Gates of Summer*? The mortification of flesh and of spirit in *The Devils*? Indeed, can any of Whiting's plays, with the single exception of *A Penny for a Song*, be described as uplifting or even, in any conventional sense, morally affirmative?

I believe they can: for even in their assertions of in-consequence they challenge, provoke doubts, and engage an audience in an agonising debate—the grounds of its dia-

lectic shifting from play to play as if the dramatist himself
were trying out an argument from a new perspective. The
stimulus of Whiting's work thus tends to be in the intensely
rewarding cerebral concentration it demands—concentration alike on the words of the text and the stage pictures that
frame them. And just as the stage pictures are too carefully
composed to intend or achieve deception, so also are the
actions of the plays enclosed within the quotation-marks of
Whiting's self-aware narrative technique. Almost always one
is aware of his distinctive, austere tone of voice, and of the
emotional shadow which it casts between a speaker and his
words. Paradoxically, it asserts both Whiting's own feeling
of dissociation and—in this expression of personality—his
presence in his plays: for this is not the mark of the auto-
biographically inclined writer, but of one entirely conscious
of the shadow he casts—as a dividing-line between the
dramatist and the drama as between the actor and the
action. It is also, I think, the line of necessary withdrawal—
such as preserves the condemned man from a consciousness
of mortality that would otherwise be insupportable.

Six years before Whiting's death, Kenneth Tynan wrote
of the dramatist himself in just these terms:

> I felt I was in the presence of a condemned man. There
> was resignation in the very set of his gentle, scolded face,
> and the expression in his large, dark eyes seemed to antici-
> pate, even to embrace defeat.[45]

There was an intended irony here, gentler than its tragic,
retrospective sting: but the image does, unmistakably, fit
the living author of the plays. Their prevailing philosophy is,
indeed, one of resignation in the face of disillusion and
despair: but the pessimism is qualified by the resignation,

and its attempted definition—the quest for a kind of contemporary stoicism—is dramatically at the heart of Whiting's achievement.

When the Council of State is debating Grandier's case in *The Devils*, De Condé makes a plea to his implacably hostile colleagues not for clemency, but for dignity in the matter of the priest's condemnation:

> For the love of Jesus Christ, if you wish to destroy the man, then destroy him. I'm not here to plead for his life. But your methods are shameful. He deserves better. Any man does. Kill him with power, but don't pilfer his house, and hold evidence of this sort against him. What man could face arraignment on the idiocy of youth, old love letters, and the pathetic objects stuffed in drawers or at the bottom of cupboards, kept for the fear that one day he would need to be reminded that he was once loved? No. Destroy a man for his opposition, his strength or his majesty. But not for this! [197]

And the fear of death not for itself but for its inconsequence —and the inconsequence in life that ill-prepares man for the loneliness of his death—is, of course, a recurrent theme in Whiting's plays—as, indeed, is the confrontation of his characters with "the pathetic objects stuffed in drawers or at the bottom of cupboards". The grocer's wife, dangling helplessly before her fatal fall in *Conditions of Agreement*; Stella's lonely, almost incidental death in *Saint's Day*; a soldier's confrontation with his inhumanity and absurdly mistaken belief in its redemption in *Marching Song*; a cripple's vain attempt to make human contact through an act of unmotivated cruelty in *A Walk in the Desert*; and a priest's humiliation of his own flesh in *The Devils*: all betoken not an

awe of evil or of death *as such*, but a terror of the inconsequence in life they confirm.

In the confessedly seminal *Saint's Day* Stella first expresses
this. "True lovers", she says, share

> a fabric of memory which will serve them well in their life
> after death when they will be together but alone. They are
> wise, for that is the purpose of any memory—of any
> experience—to give foundation to the state of death.
> Understand that whatever we do today in this house—this
> damned house—will provide some of the material for our
> existence in death and you understand my fear. [114–15]

The purpose of experience is to "give foundation to the state
of death"—and, many years and almost a life's work later,
comes Grandier's confession that he is "a dead man, compelled to live", seeking some "short-cut" to self-destruction.
[184] Such a fulfilment Sister Jeanne has herself glimpsed: it
is, she has claimed, "the glory of mortality, the purpose of
man: loneliness and death". [186] The difference, of course,
is that it is not in her death but in Grandier's that this
purpose is to be fulfilled, whereas Stella is speaking her own
epitaph: for Sister Jeanne is one of those instruments—
sometimes, as in *Saint's Day* and, maybe, in *Marching Song*,
dispassionate, but sometimes (as here) inextricably involved
in the circumstances they engineer—by means of which
Whiting confronts an individual with his mortality. Whether
this confrontation results from a profound personal dilemma,
as in *Marching Song*, or from a practical joke, as in *The
Devils*, makes little difference: ultimately, man's salvation
is within himself, his death not a means to glory but merely
the time of taking stock.

This is not to say that Whiting's work does not develop

philosophically—it does, precisely in the relative emphasis it places on the processes of living and of dying. Whiting was fond of quoting a remark of Montherlant's about the significance of character as opposed to action in drama:

A play does not interest me unless the external action, simplified as much as possible, is only a pretext for the exploration of man; unless the author has undertaken, not to imagine and put together a mechanical plot, but to express activities of the human soul with the greatest truthfulness, intensity and depth.[46]

Whiting achieves his own exploration of the human soul not by simplifying his external actions but by *abstracting* them from the "real" issues—or by making the "real" issue so demonstrably insignificant in itself that it focuses the liberated attention upon the "activities of the human soul". Thus, unmotivated cruelty and practical joking become both an *expression* of purposelessness—a precarious foundation indeed for our "existence in death"—and a *means of directing attention* to the "exploration of man".

Death is fortuitous—Paul Southman, told of Stella's, describes it as "not a very good joke", [141] and this might serve as a verdict on Grandier's besides—as are most other physical and sexual activities of human kind, which puts off childish things only to "sit together in the sun and talk of clownish things". [197] The wilfully cruel child becomes the professional buffoon, but even the circus clown erects an elaborate defence of superstition and taboo to protect himself, like the child, from the unknown. Thus, Peter Bembo in *Conditions of Agreement*, hates A.G. only because the grocer has shed tears during his circus act—as he might have stepped on the cracks between paving-stones. Rupert Forster in *Marching Song* comes face to face in battle with a boy soldier blowing a whistle, whose death teaches him that war is not just the shuffling of a pack of cards in a children's game. And the lovers Caroline and Hogarth in *The Gates of Summer* "never get out of the nursery where everything finishes broken up". [17]

This curious complex of associations with childhood and childish things is only the most insistent of the recurrent motifs in Whiting's plays. Birthdays—it is even Henry Bevis's thirty-fifth birthday in *The Gates of Summer*—also have, as Peter puts it in *A Walk in the Desert* "a sense of mystery" for Whiting. Characters share not only the enigmatic nomenclature in which their creator delighted, but also an odd ability to stand back apace from themselves—to describe their own actions as if they were somebody else's. Some of them have a habit of thinking that others are in fact dead when they are alive—A.G. of Bembo, the outside world of Paul Southman, Dido of Forster—or alive when dead, as Jonathan believes of Jesus. Settings are either of decayed grandeur—as in *Conditions of Agreement* and *Saint's Day*— or of an actual grandeur in which festers a less tangible decay, as in *Marching Song* and *The Gates of Summer*. And even such a simple object as a bicycle is employed a second time as a visual motif when, after contributing to that opening impression of incongruity in *Saint's Day*, it heralds Basilios's triumphal entry in *The Gates of Summer*.

Whether in this slight coincidence of stage props or in the pervasive insistence upon associations with childhood, surely such repetitions have common origins in Whiting's use of "people, places, things, even ideas and quotations from literature which have a personal significance put together to form a whole".[47]

If so, the dramatic implications are twofold, and contain an apparent contradiction: for these elements at once *personalise* the plays, in that they make them intensely and unmistakably Whiting's own, and *depersonalise* them, in so far as such trappings set the characters apart from their actions—or, in the terms of Montherlant's definition, make clear that the actions are "a pretext for the exploration of man". (This is the importance, too, of Whiting's use of what he called "significant coincidences" in plotting—such as Peter Bembo's prior acquaintance with A.G. in *Conditions of Agreement*, or the climactic discovery in *Saint's Day* that the little girl dancing as the curtain falls is called Stella.)

In these ways Whiting forged his own equivalent to that "line of communication" with the past which Rupert Forster described to Cadmus in *Marching Song*:

An army's line of communication is both its strength and its weakness. It stretches back sometimes broad and firm, sometimes fine and worn to base. It is not a steady supply. It pulses like a human vein according to need. Yet it must always be kept open. It must always be kept alive. In war I have struck so far forward that the line back has been stretched until it is invisible to all eyes but mine. For it is not always a thing you can mark on a map—you can't neatly signpost it for everyone to follow. You can only feel it in your belly like homesickness. It is what makes an isolated group fight its way out of an apparently impossible situation. Faith that there's a way back. . . .

A man is an army, a striking offensive force. Each one of us has the line of communication stretching out. With some of us it is weak and with some of us it is strong according to our courage. The line goes back to other people, places and ideas. From you and Catherine back into the past: from myself and the girl out to the imme-

diate happening. But we all call it by the same name,
don't we, Cadmus? Love. And as long as that line remains
open we have to live. [299-300]

"The line goes back to other people, places and ideas."
Whiting must surely have been echoing these words, consciously or unconsciously, when he was trying to describe his
own technique. Equally he must have been aware that the
actual "line of communication" Rupert had kept open—the
goat-herd's song—was illusory. Yet even so, Rupert is not
alone among his characters in affirming, quite simply, that
the hope or reality of love is the only means to salvation.
Stella's poignant envy of "true lovers" in *Saint's Day*,
Hogarth's ironic celebration of "the dark girl, the ideal
born in the garden" in *The Gates of Summer*, and the very
different sexual failures of Peter in *A Walk in the Desert*
and of Grandier in *The Devils*—all express the belief that love
is the one line of communication that, kept open, is a cause
for life but, severed, becomes a sentence of spiritual death.
    Although none of Whiting's *grandes dames*—Emily in
Conditions of Agreement, Catherine in *Marching Song*, Sophie in
The Gates of Summer, "made to purge us by pity and terror"
as she was [33]—matter anything like as much as their first
act prominence seems to anticipate, in each play the female
dominance shifts theatrically to the younger woman—to
Patience, Dido and Caroline respectively. Of course, many
of Whiting's characters tend to spawn spiritual progeny in
this way: but that such patterns of behaviour and character
do recur suggests as much a thematic as a technical preoccupation—and it is one that is explored specifically from
the woman's point of view in *Saint's Day*, and from the man's
in *A Walk in the Desert* and *The Devils*. Whether in the hopeful
companionship of Patience, the curious estrangement of

Stella, the controlled pity of Dido, the indulgent passion of Caroline, the line of communication stretches out. Yet the only "true lovers" in Whiting's plays are Edward Sterne and Dorcas in *A Penny for a Song*—and *their* truth is put to the test of a probably final parting. In Whiting's more characteristic works, the problem is rather one of how the individual is to be reconciled with himself when the quest for love— at last, the utterly lonely Peter's in *A Walk in the Desert* and the sated, unsatisfied lecher Grandier's in *The Devils*— has finally to be abandoned.

In their isolation these characters experience, like so many of their predecessors, an inward-turning of sensibility. And for the spiritual and mental cripples, this becomes a vicious circle that sends out tangents of hatred (or merely of spite) against others. Their dilemma is as Peter expresses it to Tony in *A Walk in the Desert*:

If you live as I do it all goes into your head. All the devils. And it's all thought, no feeling. (*He has groped for this word.*) Saints. Nomads. Me. What other people experience . . . all that just goes to the head and becomes a possibility. It sometimes gets pretty crowded up there with maybes. I'm trying to explain. . . .

She was standing there on the step. And I didn't feel anything. Some common tart come to the wrong house. Then I saw her . . . saw her . . . as I said. And I remembered a song. From years ago. I was once in love, believe it or not. Keep me to the point, for God's sake. So there she was. Enquiring. Unknown. And I wanted her to feel something about me. Recognise me, I suppose. . . . Something positive. It's not often now that people approach me. Either by chance or wish. There she was. I wanted to be remembered by someone. With hatred?

Why not? How can I ask for love? And it was meant to
be a joke. At first. [122]

Irresistibly, the word recurs: a joke. Played by the likes of
Peter—the cripples, for whom the lines of communication can
no longer be kept open by love. "All the devils", as opposed
to the "saints" and the "nomads"—and Whiting, his *Saint's
Day* celebrated and his *Devils* exorcised, even left a play called
The Nomads unfinished at the time of his death, retracing yet
another of those patterns that link his work into an inex-
tricable whole.

He wrote for an elite, yet portrayed always the decadence
of the elite. He evoked the irrationality of the baying mob
(in *Saint's Day*, *Marching Song*, *The Gates of Summer* and, of
course, in *The Devils*), yet also created his most sympathetic,
most nearly fulfilled characters from Patience's orphanage,
from the cottage of the child Stella, from Dido's slums—
even, less successfully but revealingly, from the Sewerman's
sewers. He sought for resignation elevated into stoicism, yet
affirmed that love was the only viable line of communication. He explored character through incongruous, often
ridiculous actions, yet made these actions so assured in their
logical self-sufficiency that they seemed, after all, to *matter*.

But when Whiting failed in this search for self-containment
—as he arguably did in *Marching Song* and surely did in
The Devils—he focused attention too directly upon that
private mythology which resolved many of the seeming
paradoxes of his work—for the playwright, if not always for
his audience:

I have written a play from remembering a gratuitous act
of cruelty which I committed when I was a child. I have
written another from a sudden moment of understanding

on seeing a man's face during a war trial. . . . I have written a comedy for no better reason, and is there a better reason, than to make a friend laugh.[48]

These are the "things given" described by Whiting in "The Art of the Dramatist", fixing what he had earlier called the "moment when" of an action—and it's an easy enough matter to attribute each of these moments to its appropriate play. Elsewhere, he wrote that it was the writer's private mythology

which prevents the play becoming mere bombast, or journalism. If we are normal human beings, we live surrounded by terrors, clowns, dead loves and old fears, represented by, say, a painting on a wall, some reels of photographic negative, a rose garden and a call from another room.[49]

What some of these motifs meant in Whiting's personal life we shall probably never know, but again we recognise instantly what most mean *in the plays*. And there they take on their own significance, and an allusiveness that often contributes, in practice, to that certain feeling of abstraction already remarked. Thus, although Whiting's best work interacts with one's own private mythology of memories, loves and fears, the effect is one almost of depersonalising the action as such. And this slight but vital distance that separates the actor from the action, the speaker from his words, makes the plays in the traditional sense moralities—that is to say, their characters embody an action in which, as Whiting himself put it, circumstances react upon character rather than *vice-versa*.[50]

This is particularly clear in the earlier plays, and it

F

influences, too, the relative significance one attaches to a character's motives and feelings—often slight, for there is little room for such ready but easy identification as can be felt for, say, the pain suffered by Grandier in *The Devils*. Rather, Whiting's best plays are parables, infinitely extensible rather than particular in reference, paradigms of human behaviour rather than enquiries into its idiosyncrasies—though these may be superficially prominent. Again, in a word, they are moralities.

Because the plays are paradigmatic, the range of decisions and choices within any given situation is infinite. If Whiting is, essentially, a teller of tales, it is *because* his characters thus define themselves through their particular and individual choice of actions—through *what they do*. Through the sum of a man's actions he creates himself. In short, existence precedes essence: and this existential quality is very much a part of Whiting's work, giving it both its potential optimism and its apparent pessimism, and adding up, of course, to yet another paradox—of a morality playwright whose morality happens to be existential. This paradox, however, is more apparent than real. If the circles of the plays are closed, the options for humankind are always open. For every lonely woman, even lonelier in death, there is the small child, her namesake, dancing hesitantly to a raucous trumpet.

"The purpose of art is to raise doubt: the purpose of entertainment is to reassure." The doubts, ultimately, are those that confront everyman in the act of accepting responsibility for his actions—for what he makes himself. And yet, in a manner that has made Whiting's plays so unacceptable to those who wish only to be entertained, this also offers a certain reassurance—the reassurance of one man's affirmation of his humanity in his art.

APPENDICES

Notes and References

Works of which fuller details are given in the Bibliography are here cited by their short titles only.

1 This was especially apparent during the controversy caused by the critics' denunciation of *Saint's Day*, after it had been awarded first prize in the Arts Theatre's Festival of Britain play competition. See the letters to *The Times* signed by Peter Brook and Tyrone Guthrie on 12th September 1951, and by Peggy Ashcroft and John Gielgud on 26th September 1951.

2 On Pinter, see Whiting's review of the published scripts of *The Birthday Party* and *The Caretaker*, reprinted in *The Art of the Dramatist*, 188–9. On Arden, see the review of the script of *Serjeant Musgrave's Dance*, *ibid.*, 164–5.

3 Thus, it is interesting to compare Whiting's general remarks about Wesker's "highly dangerous ideas" in the interview in *Theatre at Work*, 34, and his dispraise of *Roots* in a review of the published script reprinted in *The Art of the Dramatist*, 163–4 and 166–7, with his favourable response to the production of *The Kitchen*—"a fine piece of work, brief and vivid"—in *John Whiting on Theatre*, 29–37.

4 See, for example, his Introduction to *The Plays of John Whiting*, 1957, vii–ix.

5 In "From a Notebook, 2", 1961, reprinted in *The Art of the Dramatist*, 155.

6 On the unfinished plays, see further the Conclusion. A full list of Whiting's screenplays and treatments can be found in the Bibliography.

7 See the Introduction to *The Plays of John Whiting*, vii–ix. Whiting goes on to note that a play "has not the formality of music to preserve it. It cannot have the deep personal meaning of poetry. Only on the printed page, which is really an embryo state, does it retain for the writer the significance and quality of a personal act."

8 Since this chapter was written, I have had the chance to reconsider *The Birthday Party* in some detail, and I am now not at all sure that Pinter's play *isn't* written chiefly from the points of view of Goldberg and McCann. I have let my original contrast stand, however, since it is more generally accepted, and so doesn't demand demonstration: but I shall be discussing this point in detail in my study of Pinter's plays in the present series. Meanwhile, if the reader has come to my own revised conclusion, the resemblance between *Conditions of Agreement* and *The Birthday Party* can only become for him, as it has for me, even more remarkable.

9 But, discussing the then unperformed and unpublished *Conditions of Agreement* in the interview in *Theatre at Work*, 22, Whiting remarks that he had written one play before *Saint's Day*, and recently "rewrote it as a television play. The critics said, 'What on earth is he doing? He's forty something and he's writing like a twenty-eight year old.' They were dead right, of course. I changed a good deal, but I couldn't get away from the basic thing."

10 See, for example, Irving Wardle's review in *The Times* of

the play's first production in Bristol in 1965, cited in the *Collected Plays*, I, 3. "If any play of his pre-figures the comedy of menace it is this unknown early piece. . . . The affinity with Pinter is particularly close."

11 See the Introduction to *The Plays of John Whiting*, vii.

12 See the interview in *Theatre at Work*, 22–3.

13 It should perhaps be emphasised that the parody was entirely conscious on Whiting's part—indeed, one aspect of the "technical exercise" Whiting set himself in *Saint's Day*. See the interview in *Theatre at Work*, 24.

14 See the Introduction to *The Plays of John Whiting*, viii.

15 See the interview in *Theatre at Work*, 26. "Well, any name *can* be laden with significance . . .", Whiting remarks. "I like a sort of euphony, and before I start a play, I run through the names to make certain that the Christian names or the surnames are not all one, two or three syllables. Dido, Catherine, Rupert, John, Harry—so that you get a sort of pattern. . . . I don't think there is any greater significance to my use of names than that."

16 In the *Collected Plays*, I, 250.

17 See the Introduction to *The Plays of John Whiting*, viii.

18 Ronald Hayman's "Notes on the Revised Version", in the *Collected Plays*, I, 246–50, helpfully synopsises the chief revisions, and quotes extensively from them.

19 See the Introduction to *The Plays of John Whiting*, viii.

20 The edition published in the Hereford Plays Series, 1964, fully cited in the Bibliography, prints the full text of the revised version.

21 See the Introduction to *The Plays of John Whiting*, viii. Whiting is answering charges that the play's philosophy is "childish and puerile". Perhaps, he adds, Christian charity "now falls into such categories. I cannot tell."

22 The poem is reprinted in full in the *Collected Plays*, I, 253.

23 See the Introduction to *The Plays of John Whiting*, viii.

24 The story of *Saint's Day* was, Whiting claimed, "very simple. The theme, which is self-destruction, is developed on other lines and with greater clarity in the later play, *Marching Song*." *Ibid.*, vii.

25 Quoted in Ronald Hayman's "Introductory Note" in the *Collected Plays*, I, 253.

26 "Rupert has needed a life-line to survive; Harry has needed a life-lie." See Hayman's *John Whiting*, 1969, 65.

27 See the interview in *Theatre at Work*, 25.

28 *Ibid.*, 29.

29 See Samuel Beckett, *Waiting for Godot*, London: Faber, 1965, 48.

30 See the interview in *Theatre at Work*, 28.

31 See Hayman's *John Whiting*, 90–1.

32 See the Introduction to *The Plays of John Whiting*, viii.

33 See Aldous Huxley, *The Devils of Loudun*, London: Chatto and Windus, 1961.

34 "It had to be a costume play. Peter intended this—whatever it was—to be the first new play in the Aldwych venture, and he felt that a modern-dress drama would have been too great a break with the rest of the repertoire." See the interview with Richard Findlater, reprinted in *The Art of the Dramatist*, 172.

35 See the interview in *Theatre at Work*, 28.

36 *Ibid.*, 29.

37 See Gabrielle-Martina Robinson, *The Development of the Dramatic Art of John Whiting and a Comparative Study of his Major Plays*, unpublished Ph.D. Thesis, University of London, 1968.

38 See "What the Theatre Means to Me", in *Plays and Players*, I, 11, August 1954, 7. This "letter" is not reprinted in *The Art of the Dramatist*.

39 *The Art of the Dramatist* also contains "Notes for a Lecture", 1951, 71–6, and "A Lecture at Vaughan College, Leicester", 1958, 77–81.

40 See Kenneth Tynan, "The Purist View", in *Curtains*, London: Longmans, 1961, 165–7.

41 This is reprinted in *The Art of the Dramatist*, 149–54, as are a number of book reviews and other occasional pieces written between 1956 and 1960.

42 Ronald Hayman discusses the difference between Tynan's position and Whiting's in his *John Whiting*, 95–8.

43 See "George Bernard Shaw", in *The Art of the Dramatist*, 177–9.

44 See "A New English Theatre", in *The Art of the Dramatist*, 163–7.

45 See Kenneth Tynan, *Curtains, op. cit.*, 166.

46 Quoted in "A Conversation", in *The Art of the Dramatist*, 111.

47 See the Introduction to *The Plays of John Whiting*, viii.

48 See the title-lecture in *The Art of the Dramatist*, 88–9.

49 See "From a Notebook", in *The Art of the Dramatist*, 124.

50 See the title-lecture in *The Art of the Dramatist*, 93.

John Whiting

1917 15th November. Born in Salisbury, Wiltshire, son of an army captain.

1918 His father starts a legal practice in Northampton on his discharge from the Army.

1930 Sent to Taunton School.

1934 Left school, and to train at the Royal Academy of Dramatic Art, London.

1935 His first job in the theatre, with the Bankside Players at the Ring, Blackfriars.

1937 Left R.A.D.A., and after various small acting roles joined the New Garden Theatre company at Bideford, Devon.

1938 With the Croydon Repertory Company.

1939 Second World War. Served in anti-aircraft section of the Royal Artillery. Commissioned in 1942 and demobilised in 1944.

1940 Married the actress Jackie Mawson, with whom he had worked in Bideford.

1945 Returned to his acting career, playing seasons in repertory at Peterborough and Harrogate. Began to write, completing the unpublished novel *Not a Foot of Land.*

1946 Death of his father, and birth of the first of his four children. Acted at Lyric Theatre, Hammersmith, and began to write for radio: *Paul Southman* broadcast.

1947 Working in repertory with the York Repertory Company, with whom he also played at Scarborough.

1949 Broadcasts of two of his stories, *Stairway* and *Valediction*, and of the radio plays *Eye Witness* and *The Stairway*. Completed *Saint's Day*, and began work on *A Penny for a Song*.

1951 London productions of *A Penny for a Song* at the Haymarket, and of *Saint's Day* at the Arts Theatre Club, where the play was awarded the first prize of £700 in the club's Festival of Britain play competition. Began work on *Marching Song*. Joined John Gielgud's company at the Phoenix Theatre, where he played in *The Winter's Tale, Much Ado About Nothing* and (at the Lyric, Hammersmith) in *Richard II*.

1952 Began to write for films, completing three treatments for Group Three—*One Touch of Larceny, Love on Paper* and *The Golden Legend of Shults*.

1953 Began writing *The Gates of Summer*, which closed on tour before reaching London in 1956. Apart from the one-acter *No Why*, Whiting did no more original work for the live theatre until 1960, but completed three translations and worked on nineteen films during this period.

1954 Joined the Drama Panel of the Arts Council. London production of *Marching Song*.

1956 Moved to Duddleswell Manor, near Nutley, Sussex.

1957 Wrote the one-acter *No Why*, commissioned by Peter Hall as a curtain-raiser to Whiting's translation of Anouilh's *Traveller Without Luggage*, but not staged until 1964.

1960 Commissioned by Peter Hall to write *The Devils*. *A Walk in the Desert* transmitted by BBC Television.

1961 London production of *The Devils*. Became theatre critic of *The London Magazine*.

1962 Fell ill during the winter, and began to undergo treatment for cancer.

1963 Died on 16th June.

Cast Lists

A Penny for a Song

Directed by Peter Brook. Designed by Rowland Emett.
First London performance of this original version at the
Haymarket Theatre on 1st March 1951.

William Humpage	..	..	George Rose
Pippin	..	..	Joy Rodgers
Sir Timothy Bellboys	..	..	Alan Webb
Samuel Breeze ..	..	..	Denis Cannan
Lamprett Bellboys	..	..	Denys Blakelock
Hester Bellboys ..	..	..	Marie Löhr
Dorcas Bellboys ..	..	..	Virginia McKenna
Hallam Matthews	..	..	Ronald Squire
Edward Sterne ..	..	..	Ronald Howard
Jonathan Watkins	..	..	Derek Rowe
George Selincourt	..	..	Basil Radford
Joseph Brotherhood	..	..	Kenneth Edwards
James Giddy ..	..	..	Peter Martyn
Rufus Piggott ..	..	..	Alan Gordon

A Penny for a Song

Directed by Colin Graham. Designed by Alix Stone. First London performance of this revised version at the Aldwych Theatre on 1st August 1962.

William Humpage	.. ..	Newton Blick
Sir Timothy Bellboys	.. ..	Marius Goring
Samuel Breeze	.. ..	Colin Jeavons
Lamprett Bellboys	.. ..	James Bree
Hester Bellboys	.. ..	Gwen Ffrangcon-Davies
Hallam Matthews	.. ..	Michael Gwynn
Dorcas Bellboys	.. ..	Judi Dench
Pippin	.. ..	Margo Andrew
Edward Sterne	.. ..	Mark Eden
A Small Boy	.. ..	Robert Cook
George Selincourt	.. ..	Clive Morton
Joseph Brotherhood	.. ..	Robert Webber
James Giddy	.. ..	Roger Swaine
Rufus Piggot	.. ..	Henry Woolf

Saint's Day

Directed by Stephen Murray. Designed by Fanny Taylor.
First London performance at the Arts Theatre Club on
5th September 1951.

Paul Southman	Michael Hordern
Stella Heberden	Valerie White
Charles Heberden	Robert Urquhart
John Winter	Scott Harrold
Robert Procathren	John Byron
Giles Aldus	Donald Pleasence
Christian Melrose..	Ralph Michael
Walter Killeen	Robert Mooney
Henry Chater	William Morum
The Child	Peggy Palmer
Judith Warden	Anne Padwick
Thomas Cowper	Bertram Shuttleworth
Women of the Village	Judith Nelmes
	Maureen Moore
	Sabina Ward

Saint's Day

Directed by David Jones. Designed by Andrew and Margaret Brownfoot. First performance of this revival at the Theatre Royal, Stratford East, on 10th May 1965. This production transferred to the St. Martin's Theatre on 21st June 1965.

Stella Heberden	..	..	Sheila Allen
Charles Heberden	..	..	Barry Justice
Paul Southman	..	..	Michael Hordern
John Winter	..	..	Daniel Thorndike
Robert Procathren	..	..	David William
Giles Aldus	..	..	James Bree
Christian Melrose..	..	..	William Marlowe
Walter Killeen	..	..	Roger Jerome
Henry Chater	..	..	Patrick Durkin
Edith Tinson	..	..	Madge Brindley
Hannah Trewin	..	..	Margaret Diamond
Flora Baldon	..	..	Greta Wood
Judith Warden	..	..	Pamela Jackson
A Child	..	..	Christine James
Thomas Cowper	..	..	Patrick Godfrey

Marching Song

Directed by Frith Banbury. Designed by Reece Pemberton. First London performance at the St Martin's Theatre on 8th April 1954.

Harry Lancaster	Hartley Power
Dido Morgen	Penelope Munday
Matthew Sangosse	Robert Sansom
Father Anselm	Philip Burton
Catherine de Troyes	Diana Wynyard
Rupert Forster	Robert Flemyng
John Cadmus	Ernest Thesiger
Bruno Hurst	Michael David

The Gates of Summer

Directed by Peter Hall. First performance at the New Theatre, Oxford, on 11th September 1956. This production closed on tour before reaching the West End.

Sophie Faramond..	..	..	Isabel Jeans
John Hogarth	..	..	James Donald
Henry Bevis	..	..	Lionel Jeffries
Caroline Traherne	..	..	Dorothy Tutin

A Walk in the Desert

Directed by Naomi Capon. First television performance on BBC Television on 25th September 1960.

Peter Sharpe	..	..	Kenneth Haigh
Laura Sharpe	..	..	Joyce Heron
Charles Sharpe	..	..	Lawrence Hardy
Tony Coleman	..	..	Nigel Stock
Shirley Flanders	..	..	Tracey Lloyd

The Devils

Directed by Peter Wood. Designed by Sean Kenny. Lighting by John Wyckham. First London performance at the Aldwych Theatre on 20th February 1961.

Mannoury	.. .. ..	Ian Holm
Adam	.. ..	James Bree
Louis Trincant	.. .. ..	P. G. Stephens
Phillipe Trincant	.. .. ..	Diana Rigg
Jean D'Armagnac	.. ..	Patrick Allen
De Cerisay	.. .. ..	Peter Jeffrey
A Sewerman	.. .. ..	Clive Swift
Urbain Grandier	.. .. ..	Richard Johnson
Ninon	.. ..	Yvonne Bonnamy
De la Rochepozay	.. ..	Derek Godfrey
Father Rangier	.. .. ..	David Sumner
Father Barré	.. .. ..	Max Adrian
Sister Jeanne	.. .. ..	Dorothy Tutin
Sister Claire	.. .. ..	Stephanie Bidmead
Sister Louise	.. .. ..	Mavis Edwards
De Laubardemont	.. ..	Patrick Wymark
Father Mignon	.. .. ..	Donald Layne-Smith
Sister Gabrielle	.. .. ..	Patsy Byrne
Prince Henri de Condé	.. ..	Derek Godfrey
Richelieu	.. ..	John Cater
Louis XIII	.. .. ..	Philip Voss
Bontemps	.. ..	Stephen Thorne
Father Ambrose	.. ..	Roy Dotrice
A Clerk	.. ..	John Cater

No Why

Directed by John Schlesinger. Designed by Barry Kay. First stage performance as part of a programme entitled *Expeditions One* at the Aldwych Theatre on 2nd July 1964.

Jacob	..	..	..	..	Garry Van de Peer
Henry	..	..	..	..	Tony Church
Eleanor	..	..	..	..	June Jago
Max	..	..	..	..	John Steiner
Aunt Sarah	..	..	..	Elizabeth Spriggs
Aunt Amy	..	..	..	Caroline Maud
Grandfather	..	..	..	Ken Wynne
First Servant	..	..	..	Mary Allen
Second Servant	..	..	..	Wyn Jones

Conditions of Agreement

Directed by Christopher Denys. First performance at the Little Theatre, Bristol, in October 1965.

Emily Doon	..	..	..	Eithne Dunne
Peter Bembo	..	..	..	Terence Hardiman
A.G.	..	..	..	..	Frank Middlemass
Nicholas Doon	..	..	..	David Burke
Patience Doon	..	..	..	Jane Lapotaire

Bibliography

WORKS BY JOHN WHITING

COLLECTIONS

The Plays of John Whiting. London: Heinemann, 1957.
  Contains *Saint's Day*, *A Penny for a Song* and *Marching Song*, together with an Introduction by John Whiting.
The Collected Plays of John Whiting, ed. Ronald Hayman. Two volumes. London: Heinemann, 1969. New York: Theatre Arts Books, 1969.
  Volume One contains *Conditions of Agreement*, *Saint's Day*, *A Penny for a Song* and *Marching Song*, together with an Introduction by Ronald Hayman. Volume Two contains *The Gates of Summer*, *No Why*, *A Walk in the Desert* and *The Devils*, together with notes and drafts for *Noman* and *The Nomads*, and a Bibliography.
John Whiting on Theatre. London: Alan Ross, 1966. [London Magazine Editions, No. 4.]
  Contains the reviews Whiting wrote as theatre critic of *The London Magazine*, fully listed under "Critical Essays and Reviews" below.
The Art of the Dramatist, ed. Ronald Hayman. London: London Magazine Editions, 1970.
  Contains miscellaneous essays, fragments, lectures and critical writings, fully listed under "Critical Essays and Reviews" below.

Separate Editions

Saint's Day. In *Plays of the Year*, Vol. 6, ed. J. C. Trewin. London: Elek, 1952. Also London: Heinemann Educational Books, with an introduction by E. R. Wood, 1963 (Hereford Plays Series).

A Penny for a Song. London: Heinemann Educational Books, with an introduction by E. R. Wood, 1964 (Hereford Plays Series). Revised version.

Marching Song. London: French's Acting Editions, 1954, and Heinemann Educational Books, with an introduction by E. R. Wood, 1962 (Hereford Plays Series). Also in *Ring Up the Curtain*, London: Heinemann, 1955; and *New English Dramatists*, Vol. 5, Harmondsworth: Penguin Books, 1962.

No Why. London: French's Acting Editions, 1961. Also in *The London Magazine*, May 1961, 52–62.

The Devils. London: Heinemann, 1961. New York: Hill and Wang, 1961. Also in *New English Dramatists*, Vol. 6. Harmondsworth: Penguin Books, 1963.

Film Writing

One Touch of Larceny. Treatment for Group Three, 1952.

Love on Paper. Treatment for Group Three, 1952.

The Golden Legend of Shults. Treatment for Group Three, 1952.

Thanks for a Lovely Day. Dialogue, for Kenwood Films, 1953.

These Are My Daughters. Treatment for Associated British, 1953.

The Ship that Died of Shame. Screenplay for Ealing, 1954.

Castle Minerva. Screenplay for Ealing, 1955.

The Good Companions. Rewriting, for Associated British, 1956.

The Golden Fool. Screenplay for Associated British, 1956.

Talk of the Devil. Screenplay for Rank, 1956.

Nya. Screenplay for Associated British, 1957.

The Captain's Table. Screenplay for Rank, with Bryan Forbes, 1957.

The Reason Why. Screenplay for Michael Powell, 1958.

The Gypsum Flower. Screenplay for British Lion, 1958.

Von Braun. Revisions, for Columbia, 1959.

The Gentleman of China. Screenplay for Columbia, 1960.

Young Cassidy. Screenplay for Sextant-MGM, 1960.

Cleopatra. Revisions, for Twentieth Century Fox.

The Bible. Work with Christopher Fry and Jonathan Griffin.

RADIO PLAYS

Paul Southman, 1946.

Eye Witness, 1947.

The Stairway, 1949.

Love's Old Sweet Song, 1950.

TELEVISION PLAY

A Walk in the Desert, 1960. Published in *Collected Plays*, Vol. Two.

TRANSLATIONS

Sacrifice to the Wind. Translation of André Obey's *Une Fille pour du Vent.* Televised in January 1954, broadcast in April 1954, and staged at the Arts Theatre in March 1955. Published in *Plays for Radio and Television*, ed. Nigel Samuel, Harlow: Longmans, 1959; and in *Three Dramatic Legends*, ed. Elizabeth Haddon, London: Heinemann, 1964.

Traveller Without Luggage. Translation of Jean Anouilh's *Le Voyageur sans Bagage.* Staged in a double-bill with *Madame de* at the Arts Theatre in January 1959. Published in French's Acting Editions, 1959.

Madame de. Translation of Jean Anouilh's adaptation of Louise de Vilmorin's *Madame de*. Staged in a double-bill with *Traveller Without Luggage* at the Arts Theatre in January 1959. Published in French's Acting Editions, 1959.

NON-DRAMATIC PROSE WRITINGS

"Fragment of a Novel", 1947. In *The Art of the Dramatist*, 15–23.

"The Honour of the Fire Brigade", 1948. *Ibid.*, 24–30.

"A Valediction", 1949. *Ibid.*, 31–9.

"Child's Play", 1949. *Ibid.*, 40–7.

"The Image of Majesty: a Narrative for Good Friday", 1962. *Ibid.*, 53–61.

"Fragment of a Play", n.d. *Ibid.*, 48–52.

"Scenario for a Film", n.d. *Ibid.*, 62–7.

INTERVIEWS

In *Encore*, VIII, 1, January–February 1961, 13–27. An interview with Tom Milne and Clive Goodwin entitled "Writer as Gangster", reprinted in *Theatre at Work*, ed. Charles Marowitz and Simon Trussler, London: Methuen, 1967, 21–35.

In *Time and Tide*, 9th March 1961, 370–1. An interview with Richard Findlater entitled "The Man who Talked about Good and Evil", reprinted in *The Art of the Dramatist*, 171–3.

CRITICAL ESSAYS AND REVIEWS

"Writing for Actors", in *The Adelphi*, Second Quarter 1952. Reprinted in *The Art of the Dramatist*, 103–10.

"A Conversation", in *Nimbus*, June–August 1953, 65–9. Reprinted in *The Art of the Dramatist*, 111–18.

"What the Theatre Means to Me", in *Plays and Players*, I, 11, August 1954, 7.

"Modern Drama and Society: Six Opinions", in *World Theatre*, IV, 4, Autumn 1955, 44.

"The Toll of Talent in a Timid Theatre", in *Encore*, III, 3, Summer 1956, 5–6. Reprinted in *The Art of the Dramatist*, 132–4.

"From a Notebook", in *International Theatre Annual*, No. 1, ed. Harold Hobson, London: Calder, 1956, 143–7. Reprinted in *The Art of the Dramatist*, 124–31.

"To the Playguehouse to See the Smirching of Venus", in *Act*, Autumn 1956, 2–3. Reprinted in *The Art of the Dramatist*, 121–3.

"A Writer's Prospect, V: The Writer's Theatre", in *London Magazine*, December 1956, 48–52. Reprinted in *The Art of the Dramatist*, 138–43.

"The Art of the Dramatist", in *Plays and Players*, V, 2, November 1957, 6–7. Excerpts from a lecture delivered on 29th September 1957 at the Old Vic, and printed in full in *The Art of the Dramatist*, 82–100.

"Half Time at the Royal Court", in *Truth*, 8th November 1957, 1264. Reprinted in *The Art of the Dramatist*, 180–3.

"*The Theatre of Bertolt Brecht*, by John Willett", in *London Magazine*, July 1959, 65–7. Book review.

"At Ease in a Bright Red Tie", in *Encore*, VI, 4, September–October 1959, 11–15. Reprinted in *The Art of the Dramatist*, 149–54, and in *The Encore Reader*, ed. Charles Marowitz *et al.*, London: Methuen, 1965, 105–10.

"*Krapp's Last Tape* and *Embers*, by Samuel Beckett; *Orpheus Descending* and *Garden District*, by Tennessee Williams; *The Balcony*, by Jean Genet; *Three Tragedies*, by Garcia Lorca", in *London Magazine*, May 1960, 87–91. Reprinted in *The Art of the Dramatist*, 184–7. Book review.

"The Masses is too Stupid for Us", in *London Magazine*, July 1960, 34–9. Reprinted as "A New English Theatre" in *The Art of the Dramatist*, 163–7. Book review.

"*The Birthday Party* and *The Caretaker*, by Harold Pinter; *Plays*, Volumes III and IV, by Eugene Ionesco; *The Blacks*, by Jean Genet; *The Possessed*, by Albert Camus", in *London Magazine*, November 1960, 93–4. Reprinted in *The Art of the Dramatist*, 188–90. Book review.

"From my Diary", in *Twentieth Century*, February 1961, 194–200. Reprinted as "From a Notebook, 2" in *The Art of the Dramatist*, 155–62.

"Inside the Asylum?" in *London Magazine*, April 1961, 65–7. Reprinted in *John Whiting on Theatre*, 7–12.

"One and One make One", in *London Magazine*, June 1961, 71–5. Review of Sartre's *Altona*, reprinted in *John Whiting on Theatre*, 12–20.

"A Good Laugh", in *London Magazine*, July 1961, 84–7. Review of *Beyond the Fringe*, reprinted in *John Whiting on Theatre*, 21–9.

"*The Kitchen*", in *London Magazine*, September 1961, 67–70. Review of Arnold Wesker's play, reprinted in *John Whiting on Theatre*, 29–37.

"*Luther*", in *London Magazine*, October 1961, 57–9. Review of John Osborne's play, reprinted in *John Whiting on Theatre*, 37–44.

"The Critic on Trial", in *London Magazine*, November 1961, 61–4. Reprinted in *John Whiting on Theatre*, 44–52. Book review.

"Time for Tragedy", in *London Magazine*, December 1961, 73–6. Review of Christopher Fry's *Curtmantle*, reprinted in *John Whiting on Theatre*, 52–61.

"Some Notes on Acting", in *London Magazine*, January 1962, 64–6. Reprinted in *John Whiting on Theatre*, 61–8.

"The Popular Theatre", in *London Magazine*, February 1962, 84–7. Reprinted in *John Whiting on Theatre*, 68–76.

"*The Cherry Orchard*", in *London Magazine*, March 1962, 69–72. Review of Chekhov's play, reprinted in *John Whiting on Theatre*, 77–85.

"The Glare of Intimacy", in *The Spectator*, 30th March 1962, 418. Reprinted as "Tennessee Williams" in *The Art of the Dramatist*, 196–8. Book review.

"*My Place*", in *London Magazine*, April 1962, 63–6. Review of Elaine Dundy's play, reprinted in *John Whiting on Theatre*, 85–93.

"Brecht in English", in *London Magazine*, June 1962, 64–7. Review of *The Caucasian Chalk Circle*, reprinted in *John Whiting on Theatre*, 93–101.

"Coward Cruising", in *London Magazine*, August 1962, 64–6. Review of Noel Coward's *Sail Away*, reprinted in *John Whiting on Theatre*, 101–8.

WORKS ABOUT JOHN WHITING

Henry Adler, "Wanamaker and Whiting", *Encore*, IV, 2, November–December 1957, 20–7.

William A. Armstrong, "Tradition and Innovation in the London Theatre, 1960–61", *Modern Drama*, IV, 1961, 184–95. On *The Devils*.

Robert Brustein, "Missed Masterpieces", *Plays and Players*, XIII, v, February 1966, 60–1 and 67. On *The Devils*.

Adrian Cairns, "The Significance of John Whiting's Plays", in *International Theatre Annual*, No. 1, ed. Harold Hobson, London: Calder, 1956, 148–52.

H. A. L. Craig, "John Whiting", *New Statesman*, 24th February 1961, 317–18.

James Ferman, "The Theatre of John Whiting", *Granta*, 24th April 1954, 23–7.

Christopher Fry, "John Whiting's World", *The Listener*, LXXII, 1964, 837–40.

Christopher Fry, "The Plays of John Whiting", *Essays by Divers Hands*, XXXIV, 1966, 141–51.

Peter Hall, "*Saint's Day*", *The Cambridge Review*, 8th November 1952.

Ronald Hayman, "John Whiting and *Marching Song*", *Nimbus*, Autumn 1954, 50–8.

Ronald Hayman, "Tragedy in the Holiday Camp: the Plays of John Whiting", *London Magazine*, September 1969, 83–92.

Ronald Hayman, *Contemporary Playwrights: John Whiting*, London: Heinemann Educational Books, 1969.

Harold Hobson, "The Involved Theatre", in *The Theatre Now*, London: Longmans, 1953, 99–109.

Jacqueline Hoefer, "Pinter and Whiting: Two Attitudes Towards the Alienated Artist", *Modern Drama*, IV, 1962, 402–8.

J. D. Hurrell, "John Whiting and the Theme of Self-Destruction", *Modern Drama*, VIII, 1965, 134–41.

Walter Lucas, "Obituary: John Whiting", *Drama*, Autumn 1963, 38–9.

Charles R. Lyons, "The Futile Encounters in the Plays of John Whiting", *Modern Drama*, XI, 1968, 283–98.

Ian Leslie Mangham, "Plays of a Private Man", *New Theatre Magazine*, VI, 2, 1965, 21–5.

Tom Milne, "The Hidden Face of Violence", *Encore*, VII, 1, January–February 1960, 14–20. Reprinted in *The Encore Reader*, ed. Charles Marowitz *et al.*, London: Methuen, 1965, 115–24.

Garry O'Connor, "The Obsessions of John Whiting", *Encore*, XI, 4, July–August 1964, 26–36.

John Russell Taylor, "Prologue: the Early Fifties", in

Anger and After, Second Edition, London: Methuen, 1969, 23–6.

J. C. Trewin, "Two Morality Playwrights: Robert Bolt and John Whiting", in *Experimental Drama*, ed. William A. Armstrong, London: Bell, 1963, 103–27.

Simon Trussler, "The Plays of John Whiting", *Tulane Drama Review*, XI, 2, Winter 1966, 141–51.

Kenneth Tynan, "The Purist View", in *Curtains*, London: Longmans, 1961, 165–7.

Raymond Williams, "*Marching Song*: John Whiting", in *Drama from Ibsen to Brecht*, London: Chatto and Windus, 1968, 316–18.